Being of beings changeless, eternal for ever and ever

**'Union'.
In this life.
The 'Whole' truth.**

Peter Luscombe

First published in the United Kingdom in 2023
by Within and Without Publishing

ISBN 978–0–9569414–3-5

Produced by The Choir Press

Being of beings changeless, eternal for ever and ever

I had a liberating, 'eureka' experience when I first realised
that God * is *nothing*.

Furthermore, because of this, God cannot ever be
modified in any way,

God is 'ever all itself,'
and not in time and space.

God has no beginning or end,
is not born, does not die.

* The word God corresponds with the word Atman

Who knows the Atman.
Knows that happiness.
Born of pure knowledge:
The joy of sattwa.
Deep his delight
After strict self-schooling:
Sour toil at first
But at last what sweetness,
The end of sorrow.

Contents

Preface

Being of beings
changeless, eternal
for ever and ever

The 3rd edition of this essay replaces the 2nd edition titled:

'God Is, Here, Now.'

I had some doubts about the previous title, since the word 'God' means different things to different people, especially if the potential reader is an atheist.

I have made the change so it will not mislead or deter any potential readers from giving this essay their consideration.

The words shown below are used throughout this essay (changing to suit the context), and each word means exactly the same.

God * Existent * Screen * Brahman * Atman
Whole * Within * Self * Reality * Consciousness.

I could have used any of these words in the original title e.g.,

'The Existent Is, Here, Now'
'The Screen Is, Here, Now' etc.

The brief introduction with it's overview of the chapters at the start should remove any preconceptions the potential reader may have and enable an informed decision to be made as to whether to read on.

Introduction

The only reason for me to write this essay is that I know 'God Is[1], and not only that God Is; but that God Is, Here, Now and I realise that I should, at least, say so.

It is possible for anyone within certain conditions, to know this.

Throughout this essay I use the word: **Existent, Brahman[2], Atman[3], Whole, Within, Self, Reality, Consciousness**, or **Screen** to correspond with this word **God** i.e., the words are interchangeable and switch from one to the other as appropriate to the context being discussed.

I recognize that many will think: who am I to say that God is? And what do I mean by God anyway? however I ask you to take the statement **'God Is, Here, Now'** as a hypothesis which you can, and I urge you must, test out for yourself.

It is not sufficient to read this essay; to accept the arguments and reasoning put forward or to believe what I have said. You must know for yourself and the only way to know; the only proof, is through personal experience i.e., **union**.

My motivation is to encourage and stimulate you to test this hypothesis out for yourself, proceeding and meditating as suggested and as described in the books referenced below.

If you do this (seriously and over time) then you too will know, through union, that God Is, Here, Now.

The most significant books, which have influenced me to write this essay, are listed in the bibliography. Words in the text marked e.g., [1, 2, 3...] refer you to the relevant endnote number in the Notes section. These endnotes I believe are well worth reading as you come across them in the text, they include additional explanatory notes and sometimes, the word's meaning as stated in the "Compact Oxford English Dictionary".

Of all the reference books/scriptures I have seen there are two which stand out above all others and which, for me, are sufficient in themselves; these two works are the **'Bhagavad-Gita'** and the **'Crest Jewel of Discrimination'**[4] (Extracts are included here and there throughout the essay).

My sincere advice is to take these books very seriously and not to consider them as merely poetical or mythical and that, because they have been written approx. 2,500 years ago, to assume that they are now out of date or irrelevant to this time (2023).

The first chapter **'God Is, Here, Now: the Hypothesis'** starts with the statement: 'There is an *existent'*. This statement is self-evident, undeniable, and obvious but I wonder how many people really think about this *existent*; who this *existent* really is; it is true that something very definitely 'IS'.

It is true that when we are born and when we are brought up, socialised and so on we are necessarily identified with the body and this physical world of the senses. The *existent* however (as explained in this essay) is not the body, senses, mind, or the intellect. The *existent* in fact is not anything at all: it simply IS. It is the 'absolute reality', infinite and eternal (not conditioned by, relative to, or dependent upon anything else, i.e., it has no parts). Whereas the 'relative reality' (this physical world of parts and their inter-relationships, including of course, the body, senses, mind, and intellect) is wholly distinct, being in fact, superimposed upon the absolute reality.

The *existent*, in this essay, is identified as **God**. It is important to accept that my use of the word **God** is just for me the word that represents **'that** which **IS'** e.g., God is not the name of an imaginary, kindly, all wise, super being with a long flowing beard and so on and most definitely not the name of a cruel all powerful warlord type who sends unbelievers to the eternal hell fire. Other words for God are listed, changing as appropriate to suit the essay's context.

An attempt is made to describe the statement: **God Is, Here, Now.**

I doubt whether this explanation is properly adequate, but very definitely the existent (God) is the *'absolute reality'*, wholly distinct from the *'relative reality'* with which we identify ourselves day to day. The *'absolute reality'* cannot be seen or described but it self-evidently exists, i.e., it 'IS'. This *'absolute reality'* is **infinite** (i.e., without limits and impossible to measure or calculate) and has no end or beginning. It is what I think of, and describe, as **'Here'**. **'Here'** is all there is, everything that is, has been and is yet to be, is **Here**. The *'absolute reality'* is also **eternal** and has no end or beginning. It is what I think of and describe as **'Now'**. **'Now'**, like **'Here'**, is all there is. Everything that is, has been and is yet to be is **'Here', 'Now'**.

In the second chapter **'No one else will, or can, do it for you'** the point is made that everyone, throughout his or her life is responsible to God for his or her own thoughts, words and actions and everyone enjoys or suffers the consequences that flow on from such thoughts, words, and actions (everyone, without exception, is subject to these laws of nature and karma). The task, which is to come to know that: 'God Is, Here, Now' is the private responsibility of each individual. When you think about it, it is self-evident, only the self can know the Self.

In the next chapter **'Preconditions'** the obvious point is made that you must have been born a human being and so have the necessary equipment i.e., the sufficiently evolved sensory organs, the autonomic and the central nervous system, spinal cord, and brain. Given that you have all these faculties in good working order, you must then want to know and be prepared to make the necessary effort to find out.

You must be able to use this human equipment you are associated with, i.e., you have to be able to think, reason, analyse and discriminate. By doing so you can thereby overcome that very deeply ingrained identification and association of yourself with your biological and physical equipment (i.e., to overcome the ego[5] and realise you are not this physical body, comprising senses, mind, and intellect).

You must undo, or neutralize, the effects of prejudice, social, cultural, religious and the other types of conditioning and indoctrination you have been, and continue to be, subjected to.

You must accept responsibility for your own thoughts, speech, and actions, and by doing this develop self-control and a high moral behaviour. This is true for anyone regardless of what may be perceived as advantages or disadvantages of birth and upbringing e.g., physique, sex, status, wealth or whatever.

It doesn't mean you have to be superhuman; of Olympian stature; that you must be able to perform heroic acts of asceticism; self-sacrifice and so on. It simply means that you must be yourself; you must be true to yourself; you must stand alone and take responsibility for your own thinking, speech and actions and maintain awareness always of the need to overcome the ego; to dissipate and overcome the false identification of yourself with the body etc.

To find the 'Self' (absolute Self) you must lose your 'self' (the relative or phenomenal self). My way to achieve this, which worked for me, was to become God centric[6]; to cultivate an evenness of vision and so become aware that God is the One undivided 'ground' equally present, (Infinitely [Here] and Eternally [Now]) within everyone and everything, comprising 'space-time'[7]. In the same way as the 'screen' is the One undivided 'ground' equally present, within everyone and everything comprising the 'film show' superimposed upon it.

The next three chapters: **'The Whole and the Parts'; 'The Book as a Creation'** and **'The Creation as a Book'** are included because they explain the conclusion, based on my references to science and philosophy and from my own reasoning and experience, that underlying this *relative reality* (the phenomenal world of the senses) there is an *absolute reality*.

In normal everyday life, it is true for everyone, that to read a book or to contemplate a painting, you must first have the faith necessary to make this effort (indeed, before you can even begin, you may have to learn how to read). To provide the motivation therefore you must have this faith or trust that your effort will result in an enriched and more fulfilled experience, so much so, that afterwards you will be very glad and grateful you made the effort and persisted with the task.

A book or painting is a public physical object i.e., it exists in the world of the senses (the perceptual field). The experience gained from reading or contemplation, however, is not in the perceptual field but is private and subjective to you alone. This process described is similar if we consider 'space-time'; the phenomenal; the perceptual field i.e., sense-data in its entirety in the same way as if reading a book or contemplating a painting. You must first have the faith and trust (that there is indeed an absolute reality) for you to make the effort to read and contemplate this 'sense-data' world; to have the determination and persistence to pass through, as it were, and so experience this absolute reality; privately and subjectively, through 'union'.

The phenomenal world of the senses, i.e., space-time (the relative reality) is a projection of parts and can be thought of as like a film show. God, (the absolute reality) can be thought of as like the 'screen' which underlies supports and reflects this film show.

To be a devotee is to read and contemplate this (public and objective) film show (the relative reality) with the aim and desire to gain the knowledge and the experience (privately and subjectively) of the screen (the absolute reality) which underlies, supports, and reflects it.

These chapters, drawing as they do on philosophy and science, describe a view of the world which gave me the faith, and so the motivation, to get out and about, walking and meditating and by these means become an established 'devotee'.

My view of the world may not interest or stimulate you in the same way; also, it is possible that I have not been clear or have not explained it well enough, however if this is the case, just skip through these chapters.

The only thing that matters is that **you test out the hypothesis** for yourself by meditating. References to science and philosophy and my thinking on this were sufficient to convince me to make the effort and so to become a devotee.

The method of meditation I followed is described in the chapters **'The Turning Point** 'and **'Yoga and Meditation'.** I should point out that I am not putting forward a scientific theory or making an intellectual argument that I hope, or need, to win. It is like the situation where you must cross a fast-flowing river, so you need to have a boat sufficiently seaworthy to carry you across. For me the understanding I obtained by considering e.g., 'Gestalt' theory (re the 'whole and the parts') and considering the process of creation (re the theory of evolution from 'big bang' up to the present day); and by reading up on the philosophy of knowledge and perception, has provided me with this boat. It doesn't matter if it has not been constructed by a master craftsman to the highest finish and specification. The boat must just be adequate enough and reasonably sound. It is not the important issue; make your own boat if necessary. It is required only to get you across the river, once across you have no further need of it.

God
Is
Here
Now: The Hypothesis

There is an **Existent**. This cannot be denied, life **IS**; you are **HERE, NOW**, reading this. That there is an existent therefore is not a hypothesis but self-evident.

God (the Existent) is **One** i.e., without a second; there being no other; undivided; ever all itself.

There are no holes in God, no boundaries, no outside, no inside, no end, no beginning. Everybody and everything lives, or has its being, in God's presence, Here, Now; whether they know it or not; believe it or not, like it or not.

So, recall that everything you think, say and do is in God's presence – the **Eternal Witness**.

God is Impersonal

Like a Screen which underlies, supports, and reflects the film show projected upon it; is impersonally present; being entirely itself; existing before the film show begins; throughout it's duration and after it has ended. Eternally unchanging.

I found this extremely reassuring since nobody is treated or valued differently, therefore I realised that however good or bad I am, or have been, relative to others, I am nevertheless superimposed upon this 'One' omnipresent Screen.

I may feel helpless and an inadequate participant in this film show but I always know that the screen is present within me and that this is true. If it were not, then I would not be here e.g., Here, Now reading these words.

I did not truly realise i.e., experience this until I started meditating and acting, as described in this essay, then I found, after making progress, it became (although the 'screen' cannot be seen, or described), as Shankara states:

"as plain to you as water held in the palm of your hand."

There is no actual barrier (assuming the necessary pre-conditions are met) preventing you or anyone from finding this screen and so merging into it and attaining to union.

A drop of water falls as rain then runs into the river and finally flows or merges into the ocean of water, its source (then it evaporates into water vapour to condense as clouds to drop as rain and so the cycle starts over again).

The 'self' (analogous to the drop of water) follows its path through life until it chooses to find it's way back into the 'Self' (analogous to the ocean of water).

There is the realisation that the 'self' is, and has always been, 'water', and whereas before you were ignorant about this, now through union this ignorance is dissolved.

The rain drop and the river are just 'Names' and 'Forms' superimposed onto or associated with water, in fact only the water is 'Real'.

In the same way as a gold bangle and a gold coin are just 'Names' and 'Forms', superimposed onto or associated with gold, in fact only the gold is 'Real'.

In space-time however i.e., in the phenomenal world, we are born and identified with the space-time world of 'Names' and 'Forms' and for us many barriers can and do exist preventing one reaching certain goals no matter how strong the desire or effort expended e.g., for me, there is a barrier which prevents me from attaining a medal as an athlete at the next Olympic games.

I simply don't have the necessary physical strength, cardio-vascular efficiency, respiratory function, in short, my equipment; the body I am associated and identified with is simply inadequate to this task, and no matter how much I might desire such a medal and so devote myself to the required specialist training. I would not, and could not, attain one.

Whereas (given the necessary preconditions are met) there is no real barrier or obstacle preventing me from attaining *union*. The only (so called) barrier to attaining *union* with God is *ignorance* and this *ignorance* ceases to exist as soon as knowledge arises e.g. As 'Shankara' often mentions, a person sees a snake but with clear vision and knowledge realises it is just a coil of rope, there never was a snake, the snake was a delusion, it was ignorance.[8]

If you desire to find God, you can. God already Is, Here, Now. The 'Kingdom of Heaven', as it is said, 'is within you' and there is no barrier that cannot be overcome. It is necessarily the case that you and **only you** can do it i.e., only the self can know the Self – the screen within.

God is also Personal.

Seemingly a contradictory assertion, yet nevertheless God is both i.e., what may be more clearly expressed as God being both transcendent (existing apart from and not limited to the physical universe) and immanent (permanently present throughout the universe).

God; the screen; the divine ground, is there for me just as God is there for you and for anyone else. By seeking to find God, I enter a relationship with God (the screen) i.e., God becomes my guide, although God does not do anything, nevertheless through my right/wrong thinking and my right/wrong actions I become open to feedback and if receptive to this, I am therefore, so to speak, guided and this guidance gradually but increasingly dissolves my ignorance and deepens my knowledge that the 'screen' (God) IS.

I relate to, and experience God as being my ever-present companion (who Is, Here, Now) and my dearest loved[9] one.

To say that God IS; is almost the only thing that can be said, this is because God is *nothing i.e., no – thing* i.e., God is not a *thing, God* has no structure, no 'parts', there is nothing to see, touch, count or detect using human senses or scientific instruments (what is called in Mahayana Buddhism the *'Clear Light of the Void')*.

I had a liberating, 'eureka' experience when I first realised that God is *nothing* and so, because of this, cannot ever be modified in any way, God is 'ever all itself' and is not in time and space; God has no beginning, no end, is not born, does not die.

Consider the film-show projected onto the screen. It is easy to realise and appreciate that the scenery, the participants, and the languages spoken, and all the other film-show elements are relevant to and entirely confined to the film show; and that, although the screen must be present (i.e., to allow the film show to be reflected and so therefore to exist); it is entirely 'other'. It is not easy for the participants born into, identified with, and playing their role within the film show to become aware that the screen is present within them and indeed, that it pervades not only them but the entire film show (equally present within).

The use of language in this essay is not an attempt to describe the screen since this cannot be done, but rather to point to it, as it were, and explain how to become aware of it and how to proceed and so eventually become absorbed into it through union.

Language is an evolved structure existing within space-time; our perceptual field (public and objective) i.e., the film-show. It is our method of communication, spoken or written. Please remember language is inadequate and not to be taken literally or interpreted to suit your ideological upbringing as so often is the case. The aim is to describe but such descriptions are analogous.

What is necessary however is that you must **know** i.e., through **experience** (of the screen within) and you must do this by yourself, through **union**. It is not adequate to know in the intellectual sense of knowing or to be able to quote scripture and verse off by heart.

On a previous page it is set down that:

God is One i.e., without a second, there being no other; undivided; ever all itself.

If this is true, and I know from experience that it is, then if you think about it, to be talking about 'me', 'you' or even to be using language at all, is illogical since there is no 'me', there is no 'you' there is only the 'existent' (or to use one of the other substitute terms: i.e. there is only the Screen, ...God, ... Brahman, ... Atman, ... Whole, ... Within, ... Self, ... Reality ... Consciousness.

I include here an extract taken from the 'Foreword' of the book 'All There Is' by Tony Parsons.

> *"There are apparently many so-called spiritual teachers, gurus and enlightened masters, and the main thrust of their message is based on the presumption that there is such a thing as a separate individual who is capable of making choices and generating effort in order to become worthy of attaining something called enlightenment. This kind of teaching is rooted in a deep ignorance about the nature of liberation, and it continuously reinforces the idea of seeking and becoming.*
>
> *But oneness does not emerge through something gained, but rather through something lost ..."*

This book is not included in the bibliography of this essay, in fact I have only come across this and other essays (www.theopensecret.com) of Tony Parsons after the event, so to speak. Before finishing this, the 2nd edition of this book (now the 3rd edition), I thought to mention his work here.

I can say I am most definitely not putting myself up to be a spiritual teacher, guru, or an enlightened master (the second chapter of this essay is called **'No one else will, or can, do it for you'** and the first words are *'The true guru (spiritual teacher) is yourself.*

I am not having an argument with Tony Parsons, but I want to make it clear that I am writing this essay from the viewpoint of having been 'me', born into 'space-time', this 'film-show'. I regarded myself as a separate individual (and was educated, conditioned, socialised, and so on to think this) I accept now that this was a life in ignorance brought about by my false identification of the 'self' with my body, senses, mind, intellect, my environment, country, language, religion and so on.

The way out of this life of being 'me' was because I made choices and made the effort to become worthy and to attain something called enlightenment, so to speak. This essay of mine may be criticised because it reinforces the idea of seeking and becoming but it was only through seeking and becoming that I became able to write this essay.

Space-Time (the 'left-right', 'back-front' and 'up-down' of space and the 'past-future' of time plus all the other possible dimensions e.g., as postulated in string theory) **is IN God but God is not IN space-time**.

When thinking of space-time as a *film show* and God as the *screen* on which it is projected or superimposed. It is easy to understand and accept that without the screen there is no ground to support and reflect the film show (indeed there would be no film show). It is also easy to accept that the screen is entirely other i.e., it is distinct; it is not a part of the film show; not 'IN' the film show.

The screen is omnipresent;[10] 'ever all itself'. The film show i.e., space-time is a projection of parts, a superimposition.

This superimposition or projection of parts results in them coming together into various relationships and then through evolution bringing about the creation of the phenomenal universe in its entirety; as it is Here, Now: including the body, sensory organs, mind, and intellect of us human beings, e.g., including you (the reader) and me (the writer).

By the very nature of things sensory organs have evolved in order to perceive phenomena or sensory objects. In the same way the mind and intellect have evolved to enable thinking and languages to be constructed.

Through these means we are able to communicate (through speech and the written word) with other human beings and to describe and explain this space-time phenomena.

This is the reason God (the screen) cannot be perceived, in itself, with the sensory organs or communicated through language, yet nevertheless IS.

God is Infinite

Another difficult word which I do not know how to define. For me it does not make sense to think of infinity in space-time terms e.g., as having dimensions extending forever e.g., left, right, up, down, front, and back and so on for all the other possible dimensions e.g., as suggested in 'String Theory.

In infinity there is no beginning, no end and **no distance**, God is always '**Here**'; nearer than near; ubiquitous, omnipresent.

To be aware of Infinity you must BE, therefore you must be HERE. It is 'HERE' that is infinite. You cannot be anywhere else; there is nowhere else. To put it the other way round: everything that is, meaning all space-time in its entirety is 'HERE' (there is nowhere else).

God is Eternal:

Eternity is not a dimension; there is no beginning or end. As is the case with Infinity, Eternity is 'Here' i.e., **NOW**, you cannot ever not be 'Here or 'Now'.

To think otherwise is just that i.e., to be thinking and therefore in your mind and therefore in space-time. To be able to think at all however, you must 'Be' and so you must be 'Here', 'Now'.

This realisation i.e., that 'God Is, Here, Now' has been of immense help to me, since at any time I can recollect this and doing so always reminds me that 'I am' and returns me to the task.

Often for example during everyday mundane activities, say reaching for the soap in the bath, I spontaneously, and without thinking, become aware that 'God is Here, Now'.

When I shut the door on leaving the house or open the door on my return home I can recall, or I can spontaneously become aware, that 'God Is, Here, Now'. This realisation is a powerful experience.

There is not an outside (or inside) to God and although there is this familiar sense of passing through an airlock or border between the outside world and home (bringing say a sense of relaxation or relief of stress etc.) there is the realisation that God is unchanged, always 'Here, Now'.

Awakened again to this, you remain aware and when, say taking your coat off; making yourself a cup of tea and so on, that all these actions are done in God's presence; change your mind and choose a mug rather than a cup you realise God remains unchanged, ever always God – the 'eternal witness.'[11]

In another space-time scenario you perceive in front of you, within your reach, two objects e.g., a tacky plastic bauble and a sparkling radiant diamond.

God is equally God whether the manifestation of God's presence (Here, Now) has the 'name' and 'form' of a plastic bauble or whether it has the 'name' and 'form' of a sparkling radiant diamond.

For the devotee, God is equally present in both and to be in God's presence is the highest experience, the devotee values and loves God and wants nothing other than to remain in this experience.

It is true there is a (space-time) difference between the plastic bauble and the radiant diamond. In the world of the senses the value of the diamond will be far, far greater than that of the plastic bauble. This can provoke a desire to possess it, perhaps for its beauty, but more likely for the money it can be turned into. This desire can be so strong that it can tempt one to steal it and even to kill someone for it.

In this scenario, the attention becomes focused solely on the diamond and all the possibilities it opens up in the imagination; to what one could do; what one could buy and so on, and there is no awareness of God's presence.

The devotee, however, holding fast to God, so to speak, doesn't suffer from the same intensity of desire and even if tempted he or she will hold fast. They (devotees) have, or are cultivating, the evenness of vision which leads them into the experience of God's presence.

You can never leave God even if you wanted to, there is not an outside, no place you can go to where God is not.

There may have been an acceptance intellectually that 'God Is, Here, Now' and an intellectual understanding that strengthened your faith in the truth of this statement, but it is as nothing compared to the actual realisation: the experience of it! Thereafter you are strengthened, knowing that you have the power to open yourself to it again by recall e.g., through meditation.

Although you cannot adequately describe it, or give an explanation which will be taken seriously by anyone else, and although there is no way you can hold or capture the experience you know however that beyond any doubt God Is.

You know that the statement: 'God Is, Here, Now' is not wishful thinking, comforting, escapist or whatever but true. There is no doubt there is an existent i.e., God is (and because of this, you are), the existent is infinite (Here); the existent is eternal (Now). This returns you to the task, to take advantage of your life to gain this knowledge and to attain union.

Extracts from my two preferred versions of the Bhagavad-Gita are included, here and there, throughout this essay, not just because they are relevant and relate to the subject but also, because they show the value of having more than one version. In fact, I used the 'Swami Prabhavananda and Christopher Isherwood' copy from the beginning i.e., decades ago. Only recently, when it doesn't matter if I ever read anything ever again, did it occur to me that other versions might give a different interpretation.

The 'Edward Arnold' version is closer to the original poetical beauty, and I was, and am, very glad to have it to read and refer to, however the copy I used from the start, decades ago helped me because of the introduction and appendix by the late Aldous Huxley who I have always respected and admired for his fine intellect.

The translation is simpler, partly prose and partly verse, which works very well for me. I recently visited Foyle's bookshop in London to look at other translations comparing them specifically against the extracts from my two versions of the 'Gita (e.g., see examples on the next page and here and there included in this book). As a result, I found myself very happy to keep with my existing two versions since other translations did not add anything to cause me to want them (albeit there are probably many other versions I have not seen).

Sri Krishna to Arjuna

Not wounded by weapons
Not burned by fire
Not dried by the wind,
Not wetted by water:
Such is the Atman,

Not dried, not wetted,
Not burned, not wounded,
Innermost element
Everywhere, always
Being of beings
Changeless, eternal
For ever and ever.

This Atman cannot be manifested to the senses or thought about by the mind. It is not subject to modification. Since you know this, you should not grieve.

Bhagavad-Gita, translated by Swami Prabhavananda and Christopher Isherwood. (Page 42)

Sri Krishna to Arjuna

I say to thee weapons reach not the life;
Flame burns it not,
Waters cannot o'erwhelm,
Nor dry winds wither it.
Impenetrable, Unentered, unassailed,
Unharmed, untouched, Immortal,
all-arriving, stable, sure, Invisible,
ineffable,
By word and thought uncompassed,
Ever all itself.
Thus is the soul declared!
How wilt thou, then –
Knowing it so – grieve when thou shouldst not grieve?

The Bhagavad-Gita translated by Sir Edward Arnold (Page 20)

Sri Krishna to Arjuna

These are the last words that I shall say to you, the deepest of all truths. I speak for your own good. You are the friend I chose and love.

Give me your whole heart,
Love and adore me,
Worship me always,
Bow to me only,
And you shall find me:
This is my promise.
Who love you dearly.

Lay down all duties.
In me, your refuge.
Fear no longer,
For I will save you
From sin and bondage

Prabhavananda and Isherwood (Page 172)

Sri Krishna to Arjuna

Nay! But once more
Take my last word,
My utmost meaning have!
Precious thou art to Me; right well-beloved!
Listen! I tell thee for thy comfort this.
Give Me thy heart! adore Me! Serve Me! Cling In faith and love and reverence to Me!
So shalt thou come to Me! I promise true,
For thou art sweet to Me!
         And let go those –
Rites and writ duties! Fly to Me alone!
Make Me thy single refuge! I will free Thy soul from all its sins! Be of good cheer!

Sir Edward Arnold (Page 182)

No one else will, or can, do it for you.

The true guru (spiritual teacher) is **yourself.** It is through your own actions and meditation that you gain knowledge and direct experience of God, Then, if you continue with constancy and devotion, eventually you will attain to full union. **No one else will, or can, do it for you**.

The truth of the matter is that you become identified with space-time, necessarily so, when you are born and as you grow up. As a human being you are dependent on your parents (and your society etc.) to nurture, safeguard, educate you and so on until you can (if this is successfully achieved) stand on your own feet, able, aware, and accepting that you have responsibility for your own thinking, speech and actions and so then proceed onwards to live your life as an independent human being.

Despite the case that parents, siblings, friends, and colleagues may constantly surround you, you are nevertheless alone. You are born alone; you live alone, and you die alone. (By using the word, **you**, I mean the phenomenal you, with which you are identified when you are born. It is the body etc. that is born, lives then dies, the whole point behind this book is to urge you to do what is necessary to realise that the real **you** is not the body. The real **you** is the **screen,** the real **you** is the **Atman,** and then realise that this **Atman** is **Brahman**).

I don't know if you have had this realisation of being alone, I can imagine it is very easy to go through one's entire life quite unaware of this, enjoying close loving relationships with relatives, friends and colleagues; constantly engaged in work and leisure activities; moving from one pleasant experience to the next (this is perhaps an ideal and unrealistic view since many do not have close loving relationships and do not enjoy an ongoing series of pleasant experiences).

In my case, at a certain point in life, I found myself in an uncomfortable situation, isolated and without any resources. It was like I was at sea, after having cut my moorings, so subsequently finding myself helplessly subject to the continuous ups and downs on the sea surface. Then in stormy weather, I became aware, and frightened by the experience of sinking and going under, but at the point where I thought all might be lost my feet touched the seabed and this changed everything.

I became grounded. I discovered that there was this solid, unchanging basis to my existence; deep within (unseen and previously not known about) it had always been there and now with this realisation, this knowledge, my fear dissipated and my whole outlook changed dramatically. I recommend that you contact this seabed, so to speak, through practicing right action and right meditation.

In actual day-to-day terms the realisation described above came when I was on the road (walking towards Bournemouth with the idea of getting a temporary seasonal job e.g., as a deck chair attendant or similar) and I moved off the road into a wood to sit down and get some rest.

It was when I was here in the wood that I realised that I was alone, not alone in the conventional sense of being lonely and isolated but in a profound, illuminating sense of being alone i.e., alone absolutely and that I had always been so, and that it could never, ever, be otherwise.

This was because I realised that everything I see and hear and everything I feel and so on comes into consciousness through my eyes, my ears, and the other senses available to me and that it could never be otherwise. It is not possible, and never will be, to see through another's eyes, and no one else can, or ever could, see through mine.

It was no longer the frightening realisation that I **am alone** in the world but rather the liberating realisation that I **alone am.** To put it more accurately that the **existent alone is,** everything else is just perception i.e., just relationships of sense data e.g., sight, sound, feelings, and other sensory information.[12]

I realised that this life is private to me and depends on how I deal with the sensory information that I receive, process, think about and interpret in my mind and on how well I use this to influence the decisions and actions I take, and so shape and create the phenomenal reality within which I live and experience e.g., if I see a rope (to use Shankara's example again) but interpret it to be a snake this will influence my future actions greatly, perhaps inducing fear and making me change direction and so avoid going near it. I therefore experience the consequences of this decision, whether they turn out to be good or bad. And so long as this mistaken identification endures, I remain in this false belief (and possibly will never discover) that in truth the 'snake' is just a 'rope'.

It immediately occurs to me that it could be argued just as easily the other way round, in that if I see a snake but interpret it to be a rope then I will not be afraid and so (losing this protective reaction) proceed and in my ignorance die from snake bite.

This is the problem with using language; it is only useful in providing an analogy.

The point I want to underline is that it is your responsibility to gain control of your mind and your thought processes, and then to use them to the best of your ability to guide your speech and your actions. The words you read in this essay enter your consciousness via your senses, for you to consider in your mind. I do not have an ulterior motive other than to stimulate you to accept the 'hypothesis' (God Is, Here, Now) and to realise, so to speak, that the snake is a rope. I am not playing any ego games. I am not trying to establish a new religion, movement, or ideology. I have no argument with scientists, atheists, or anyone. Every individual is responsible for his or her own thoughts, speech and actions and it is for everyone to realise their identity for themselves (indeed no one else can do it for you? Who else is there?).

I reiterate that it is the **existent** that **is real**, not the ego (your false self); your identification with the body, senses, mind etc. but now it predominates, and it seems overwhelmingly the case that you are a separate individual alone in a world containing millions of other separate individuals.

It is obviously true that you must get up each morning wash, dress, eat then go to work and the like. You must remain continuously engaged in these activities to maintain your health and wellbeing, your upkeep, your career, and your future life living in a society populated by other people living their own separate lives whose activities may not coincide with yours.

The way to overcome this ego is to regard your body, senses, mind, and intellect and so on as equipment with which you are closely associated and have responsibility for, and which will take you where you want to go. The so called ('Gateway to Brahman').

There is 'Freewill' (in my common sense understanding of the term) in that you can choose to 'go towards' or you can choose to 'go away' from realising your identity; i.e., choose between the **'self'** (ego) or the **'Self'** (God).

To accept that you are alone in the world (the 'I alone am' realisation as mentioned previously) is daunting but you are not alone of course since God is, and you benefit from God's grace[13], either directly or indirectly throughout your life.

During your life you receive sense data, mainly via the five sensory organs i.e., sight, sound, touch, taste & smell. The senses, I consider and write about in this essay, are sight and sound.

All sense data is passed via the central nervous system to the various specialised areas of the brain where it is sorted, processed, and related together, providing food for thinking about in your mind. These relationships of data comprise **your** perception, i.e., **your** mental representation of reality. This is **private and subjective** to **you**.

Your ideas, beliefs and day-to-day knowledge derive from the sense-data you receive and process in your mind. God cannot be seen or described by this sense-data, but you believe and have faith that God Is, imagining God to be like the screen within but beyond your perception – like the screen is within but beyond the film show. The 'One,' indivisible, absolute Reality.

In our day-to-day experience however, lived in the perceived ('space-time') world, we divide, categorise, name, and describe relationships of sense-data e.g., as physical objects having various qualities; height, width, colour, texture, length and so on and we refer to these objects as being near or far; here or there; as being public or private; objective or subjective, good, or bad and the like. This also applies to living forms including ourselves and other human beings which we identify with names and refer to as 'me' or 'you'; 'us' and 'them'; 'friend' or 'foe' and on and on. This is all vital and necessary of course to enable us to make sense of what we see and hear and to enable us to survive; to relate and to communicate with others.

By these means relationships form, survive, and evolve, civilisations, belief systems, ideologies, religions, philosophies, creative arts, music, literature and so on are created and developed. It is not the case however that this evolving creation develops necessarily in a positive manner and in our best interest. Freedom, democracy, knowledge and enlightenment and other good developments do not necessarily, or automatically, result.

Even religions (the belief in and worship of a God) since being largely manufactured and developed within this perceived ('space-time') world commit the error of overlooking the fact that the Screen, God, Atman, Brahman, Whole, Within, Self, Reality, Consciousness, (interchangeable terms) is the 'One', indivisible, unchanging, infinite, eternal, absolute Reality.

I refer particularly to those religions based on a **'Them and Us'** concept,

This **'Them and Us'** attitude is responsible for regarding people who are not assigned by birth into the religion/ideology or those who do not convert to that religion/ideology as being 'heathens' or 'infidels[14] or kaffirs'[15] to be belonging to the **'Them'** group.

The term 'heathens', I don't think is in use anymore, the term 'infidels'/kaffirs however seems to be widely used, and usually, or perhaps always, in a negative and abusive manner. The term 'atheist' is a legitimate term but isn't taken as derogatory except perhaps in those ideologies e.g., where they are considered as, unbelievers along with infidels/kaffirs.

Such, so called religions/ideologies seem to have no love of God or any understanding that God is the 'One', Indivisible, Infinite, Eternal, Here, Now, Absolute Reality; no understanding that God is equally present in all; no recognition that everyone is responsible for their own thinking, speech, and actions.

It seems to the 'Us' members of the ideology that everyone else is an unbeliever and belongs to the 'Them' group, presumably these unbelievers are regarded as like 'holes' within God; that somehow God is not present for 'Them' as God is present for 'Us'.

The so-called religion or ideology holding this 'Us and Them' attitude makes a grotesque error and shows a lack of awareness that God, the 'One', indivisible, absolute reality does not, and cannot, contain holes.

The truth is that you alone (God also of course) know whether you are a believer or not. Everything seen is seen through your eyes, you cannot see through anyone else's and similarly no one else can see through yours.

Others must see using their own eyes, relate the sense-data for themselves, and draw their own conclusions. If others believe in God, then it should inspire them to seek that knowledge and that direct experience of God for themselves remembering they are responsible for their own thinking, words, and actions.

Sri Krishna to Arjuna	Sri Krishna to Arjuna
And he who dwells. United with Brahman, Calm in mind, Not grieving, not craving, Regarding all men With equal acceptance: He loves me most dearly.	Such a one, growing one with Brahman, serene, Sorrows no more, desires no more; his soul, Equally loving all that lives, loves well Me, Who have made them, and attains to Me. By this same love and worship doth he know Me as I am....
Prabhavananda and Isherwood (Page 171)	Sir Edward Arnold (Page 180)

There is no **'Them and Us'**, this is just a very harmful and divisive unenlightened concept. How can 'God, Here, Now' i.e., infinite, and eternal, omnipresent, like the screen, be divided up, reserved for believers only (the **Us** group) but exclude the others (the **Them** group).

As already mentioned, you cannot see through anyone else's eyes. You create and occupy your own relative reality; from the relationships of sense data that enter your mind. You must be yourself, take control of yourself, take responsibility for your own thinking, speech, and actions. You are the creator and sole member of your personal and private reality. You need to recall always that God (the existent) Is, Here (Infinite), Now (Eternal) and so develop an evenness of vision and to 'see' (in the sense of becoming aware; it being not possible to see God who is formless and without parts); the 'One' in the 'Many' (the omniscient unchanging screen within, but beyond or distinct from, the ever-changing phenomenal show).

For me being a believer or a member of a religion, doesn't, of itself, mean anything since it doesn't seem to bring you into Union. For others it may be different (see note 46 re Bhakti yoga).

Religions are largely, if not wholly, man-made with all that that implies. The religion may have been founded, and developed on the teachings of say Abraham, Jesus, Siddhartha Gautama, and others but invariably those who recorded and set the story to paper, so to speak, included in their writings, additions, and embellishments to fit in with the scriptural prophecies, pagan customs and superstitions existing at that time.

The religions over time also became variously interpreted leading to disputes and divisions. Leading to sects and denominations becoming established and then leading to disputes one against the other e.g., currently, and perhaps the most extreme example, is the conflict existing between the

''Shia' and 'Sunni' Muslim branches of the Islam ideology.

So, it is apparently the case that within the (Parent) **'Us and Them'** division i.e., between Muslims (say, **'Us'** – the true believers) and everyone else (say **'Them'** – the infidels/kaffirs; the unbelievers) there is now an additional internal subdivision; this being between the 'Shia' (**Us**) and the 'Sunni' (**Them**) or vice versa. I don't know if the 'Shia' regard the 'Sunni' as unbelievers (and so presumably belong with the Infidel/Kaffir **'Them'** group) or whether the 'Sunni' regard the 'Shia' as belonging to the Infidel/Kaffir **'Them'** group, it depends, of course, on which group you happen, like it or not, to be allocated to by birth or conversion. There is also the shocking and contemptible **'Us and Them'** division within the Islam ideology that exists between men and women.[16]

I find great difficulty in understanding the reverence those brought up within the Islam ideology have towards the Quran. I find much of it to be incomprehensible. Just to consider an extract shown:

II

THE COW

In the Name of God, the Merciful, the Compassionate

This statement is repeated (variably as according to which version is read) at the start of each sura. e.g., "In the Name of Allah, the Most Beneficent, the Most Merciful"

The dictionary states 'Merciful' as showing compassion and forgiveness, or in another source as being the love that seeks to forgive, console, assist, and care for others in time of need. Mercy is an act of love done without expecting anything in return; it is done for love itself.

This sura on reading however, for me, describes God as very far from being compassionate or merciful, but rather, it seems as being vindictive. (i.e., disposed to seek revenge, marked by, or resulting from a desire to hurt; spiteful).

God, it seems creates beings and then requires them to be grateful and to be believers in him. If he created them, why did he not create them all to be grateful believers? Why does he create some to be unbelievers?

5   As for the unbelievers, alike it is to them
    whether thou hast warned them or hast not warned them,
        they do not believe.
    God has set a seal on their hearts and on their hearing,
        and on their eyes is a covering,
    and there awaits them a mighty chastisement.

        but they are not aware.
    When it is said to them, 'Believe as the people believe',
    they say, 'Shall we believe, as fools believe?'
        Truly, they are the foolish ones,
            but they do not know.
    When they meet those who believe, they say, 'We believe';
    but when they go privily to their Satans, they say,
        'We are with you; we were only mocking.'
    God shall mock them, and shall lead them on
        blindly wandering in their insolence.
15 Those are they that have bought error
        at the price of guidance,
    and their commerce has not profited them,
        and they are not right-guided.
    The likeness of them is as the likeness of a man
    who kindled a fire, and when it lit all about him
    God took away their light, and left them in darkness
            unseeing,
        deaf, dumb, blind—
        so they shall not return;
        or as a cloudburst out of heaven
    in which is darkness, and thunder, and lightning—
        they put their fingers in their ears
    against the thunderclaps, fearful of death;
        and God encompasses the unbelievers;
    the lightning wellnigh snatches away their sight;
    whensoever it gives them light, they walk in it,
    and when the darkness is over them, they halt;
        had God willed, He would have taken away
        their hearing and their sight.
    Truly, God is powerful over everything.

Why did God set a seal on their hearts etc.? Why did not God unlock the seal on their hearts and on their hearing, and why did God not remove the covering on their eyes? Why did God mock them (presumedly meaning to ridicule and deride them)? Why then lead them on (presumedly in the wrong direction) then leave them deaf, dumb, and blind? Then because they do not hear or see chastise i.e., punish them.

If man has free will then man may choose not to be a believer and can hardly be penalised for that since he is exercising his God given free will. If he has not been created with free will i.e., he is determined and therefore has no choice and cannot be considered a believer or an unbeliever. He is what he has been created to be and has no free will to be otherwise.

How does this portrayal tally or harmonise with the statement previously put forward:

God is One i.e., without a second, there being no other; undivided; ever all itself.

Such ideologies, as per the example above, operate like cults[17] their objectives, seem to have nothing to do with assisting and facilitating their members to love God; to gain unitive knowledge and the direct experience of God i.e., the **'One, Indivisible, Absolute Reality'**.

In the 'Bhagavad-Gita' (see the verse on the next page) reference is made to events in history e.g.,

In every age I come back

To deliver the holy, ...

I rise, from age to age, and take Visible shape and move a man with men, ...

These verses appearing about 500 years before Jesus Christ and Gautama Siddharth (the Buddha) came into the world.

Arjuna:	Arjuna:
Vivaswat was born long before you. How am I to believe that you were the first to teach this yoga.	Thy birth, dear Lord, was in these later days, And bright Vivaswata's preceded time! How shall I comprehend this thing thou sayest, "From the beginning it was I who taught?"
Sri Krishna:	
You and I, Arjuna, Have lived many lives. I remember them all; You do not remember.	Sri Krishna:
I am the birthless, the deathless, Lord of all that breathes. I seem to be born: It is only seeming, Only my Maya. I am still master of my Prakriti The power that makes me.	Manifold the renewals of my birth Have been, Arjuna! And of thy births too! But mine I know, and thine thou knowest not, O slayer of thy Foes! Albeit I be Unborn, undying, indestructible, The Lord of all things living; not the less – By Maya, by my magic which I stamp. On floating Nature-forms, the primal vast – I come, and go, and come.
When goodness grows weak, When evil increases, I make myself a body.	When righteousness Declines, O Bharata! When Wickedness Is strong, I rise, from age to age, and take Visible shape, and move a man with men,
In every age I come back To deliver the holy, To destroy the sin of the sinner, To establish righteousness.	Succouring the good, thrusting the evil back, And setting virtue on her seat again.
Prabhavananda & Isherwood (Page 60)	Sir Edward Arnold (Page 42)

Most people are members of a religion, or an ideology, simply because of where they were born and because of their socialisation or indoctrination. They often have no freedom to have an individual life and thoughts of their own.

To me it seems that to be born into an ('**Us and Them**') ideology is really nothing other than to be born into a kind of servitude; to have no responsibility for your own thinking, speech, and actions; but always to practice submission and obedience to the ideology (in all its various and differing interpretations).

See **Islam's Sharia law** and notes re Stoning.[18]

I looked for information on *'conversion'* e.g., say, from the Islamic ideology into another ideology or religion or to leave and become an atheist. I found broadly speaking that a person who wishes to convert out of the Islamic ideology is classified as being an 'apostate' and should be killed.

This is not the place to go into detail about this, but I found the experience of reading the commentaries from Islamic scholars, commentators, propagandists and from reading the many associated extracts from the 'Quran', to be a depressing experience.

I confess that I do not understand why this book (the Quran) is so highly thought of and suspect it is probably the result of indoctrination and socialization rather than the illumination or experience gained from reading it. To me (as an individual who has not been seriously indoctrinated, socialised, or culturally conditioned) it does not come across as being a spiritually enlightening work i.e., which inspires me and gives me knowledge and practical advice to enable me to realise God, i.e., leading me towards 'union' (the only proof of God).

At least, however it has answered the question that I have often asked myself after reading 'The Quran' (in several versions) i.e., why is the Islamic ideology so prominent? (said to comprise, according to Wikipedia, approx. 24% of the world's population).

The Bhagavad-Gita is said to be the most systematic scriptural statement of the Perennial Philosophy[19] and is relevant to all, no matter what religion/ideology they happen to be born into; whether they practice it or not, or are atheists.

The author 'Aldous Huxley' in his impressive anthology 'The Perennial Philosophy', shows that many individuals of different outlook and background, isolated from each other by geographical place and historical time have undergone similar experiences and this can be realised from their words,

e.g., in Chapter 2, ('The Nature of the Ground'),

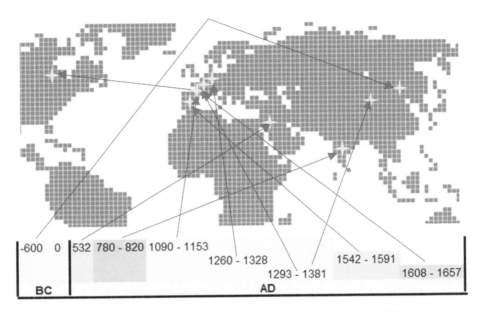

-600   0   532   780 - 820   1090 - 1153

1260 - 1328

1293 - 1381

1542 - 1591

1608 - 1657

BC

AD

Huxley includes short extracts from: St Bernard (France, 1090 -1153). Shankara (India, 788 – 820 AD). Lao Tzu (China, 6th century BC). St John of the Cross (Spain 1542 – 1591). Eckhart (Germany. 1260 – c. 1328). Ruysbroeck (? Holland, 1293 – 1381). J.J. Olier (? France or Canada, 1608 – 1657). 'The Tibetan Book of the Dead' (written 8th century buried in central Tibet, subsequently discovered in the 14th century). 'Brihad Aranyaka Upanishad' (one of the older, "primary" Upanishads, pre-mid-first millennium BCE) and Dionysius the Areopagize (probably Syrian 5th to early 6th century but written before 532 AD).

This practice of bringing together related examples continues throughout each chapter of the book. It is remarkable how such a man (Aldous Huxley) can be so thorough in his research and to put it to such good use. Included here are several examples – from Ch. 2 'The Nature of the Ground' (as space permits):

".... For in thus breaking through, I perceive what God and I are in common. There I am what I was. There I neither increase nor decrease. For there I am the immovable which moves all things. Here man has won again what he eternally and ever shall be. Here God is received into the souls".

Eckhart

"The Godhead gave all things up to God. The Godhead is poor, naked, and empty as though it were not; it has not, wills not, wants not, works not, gets not. It is God who has the treasure and the bride in him, the Godhead is as void as though it were not."

Eckhart

"O nobly born; the time has now come for thee to seek the Path. Thy breathing is about to cease. In the past thy teacher hath set thee face to face with the Clear Light; and now thou art about to experience it in its Reality in the Bardo state... in which the soul is judged – or rather judges itself by choosing, in accord with the character formed during its life on earth, what sort of an afterlife it shall have. In this Bardo state all things are like the cloudless sky, and the naked, immaculate Intellect is like unto a translucent void without circumference or centre. At this moment know thou thyself and abide in that state ..."

The Tibetan Book of the Dead

"It was from the Nameless that Heaven and Earth sprang; the named is but the mother that rears the ten thousand creatures, each after its kind. Truly, 'Only he that rids himself forever of desire can see the Secret Essences.' He that has never rid himself of desire can see only the Outcomes."

Lao Tzu

"Who is God? I can think of no better answer than, He who is. Nothing is more appropriate to the eternity which is. If you call God good, or great, or blessed, or wise, or anything else of this sort, it is included in these words, namely, He is."

St Bernard

"(In the Reality unitively known by the mystic), we can speak no more of Father, Son, and Holy Spirit, nor of any creature, but only one Being, which is the very substance of the Divine persons. There were we all one before our creation, for this is our super essence. There the Godhead is in simple essence without activity."

Ruysbroeck

"Thou must love God as not-God, not-Spirit, not-person, not-image, but as He is, a sheer, pure absolute One, sundered from all two-ness, and in whom we must eternally sink from nothingness to nothingness."

Eckhart

Preconditions

The human being (as far as I know) is the only life form that has the sufficiently evolved ability and the opportunity to gain direct unitive knowledge and experience of God (the 'One, Indivisible, Absolute Reality'). Other life forms e.g., Cat, Dog, Dolphin, Ape or whatever cannot, simply because they lack the wherewithal; the necessary equipment i.e., the sufficiently evolved Nervous System and Brain.

At some point in evolution the pre-human life form started to walk upright, leaving the hands free and so (also because the thumb opposed the fingers) able to use them, and natural objects, as tools. This great advance resulted in ever increasing development of the nervous system and brain until eventually the pre-human life form became so conscious or aware that it became aware of it's **self**.

This was the turning point in evolution; the threshold, where consciousness turned back on itself. This development differentiated the human being from all other life forms. The human being thereafter became self-aware and reflective; able to look inward and, whereas all life forms know, the human being knows that he or she knows and therefore can ask: Who am I? What is real? To reason, analyse, discriminate, and meditate, and through these means continue to evolve and so become ever more conscious.

You start from where you are whatever your circumstances might be; realizing you are '*yourself*' and therefore responsible and accountable for '*your*' thinking, decisions, speech, and actions.

You must do the right thing (in so far as you can and according to your own conscience and reasoning) not the wrong thing. This means you must be yourself, stand alone and perhaps live alone (at least I had to).

You must think for yourself with the information you have or can gather e.g., by finding out; by seeking advice; by learning from previous experience; by reading and so on e.g. I read a book: 'Crime and Punishment' by Fyodor Dostoevsky, when I was about 14, I wanted to know about life; and this man, together with others including Aleksandr Solzhenitsyn, Hermann Hesse, Aldous Huxley, George Orwell, John Steinbeck, Leo Tolstoy to mention a few, were very much the authors at that time for me and although I found reading 'Crime and Punishment' a difficult and depressing experience, I definitely felt that I was doing something valuable and to my advantage so I kept at it.

After reading this book, I knew that whatever I did in my life and however it turned out i.e., however poor, and mediocre I might be; I would not commit such a crime or go down such a route. I vowed to myself very strongly that I was going to be true to myself (and not care what others might think) and that maintaining a clear conscience was to be central to my every decision and action I would take from then on.

This decision was empowering. Another valuable realisation I gained was that Dostoevsky, alongside those other authors (who for me at the time were difficult in some ways to read), was a great author because he could communicate **"What it is like"** e.g., to have killed someone with an axe; to be a prisoner in a Gulag, and similarly what it would be like, in all sorts of situations and actions, but yet being spared having to go through the actual experience yourself. Admittedly this being in a virtual or simulated manner but still a very effective means of broadening and deepening the mind.

In 'War and Peace' by Leo Tolstoy the main hero, for me, was Pierre and at a certain point in the story when he was describing the (pistol) duel, I had a powerful experience of 'what it was like to be Pierre'. Time and space for me seemed to disappear; it was like I was there, even though the account of the duel was written about 150 years ago in Moscow about

1,500 or so miles distant from where I was reading about it, at home in Exeter, England.

It was one of the first experiences for me that the 'Self' within me was no different to the 'Self' that was within Pierre or rather within the author Tolstoy, (since Pierre was his fictional character). The 'Self,' as it were, is timeless and eternal (i.e., the 'One'); the Absolute Reality; equally the same within all. The phenomenal details e.g., concerning time, place, scenery, backdrop, and such like are the ever changing, finite, transient details (i.e., the 'Many').

Returning to the realization that you are yourself and therefore responsible and accountable for your own thinking, decisions, speech and actions, it necessarily requires you, on frequent occasions, to put your personal interests to one side (I believe this does not mean to reduce yourself to penury), for me anyway I have always felt it important to look after yourself because only then, so to speak, will you be in the position where you are able to look after, or be useful, to others.

To put it another way, I believe it's very important to eat to live, rather than to live to eat; everything in moderation; to nothing be attached, and so on. Although these are seeming platitudes, they do have real meaning and relevance.

You do need to support your body (the equipment you have been associated with at birth); to maintain and satisfy its basic needs (food, water, shelter, warmth. . .).

You do need to take account of, and to deal with, the many desires that arise and are stimulated by activity of the senses and changes in your blood chemistry, e.g., the release, ebb and flow of hormones and other products directly into the blood which often stimulate your thinking and fantasising (fanning the flames, so to speak).

There is therefore the very important need to exercise self-control this partly, if not wholly, can be achieved through the process of sublimation i.e., by redirecting or transforming that energy which otherwise becomes consumed in satisfying your desires, sexual energy especially.

So do this by offering everything to God i.e., love God with all your heart and all your mind. I read somewhere that the best way to remove all the blue ink from an ink bottle is to continuously pour in water, at first it seems to make everything much worse, the water goes in and then comes out blue, however eventually the ink is diluted, then more and more so, until it ceases to be and thereafter the water coming out is as pure and clear as that going in, the state of union and fullness replaces that of separation and desire; love loves love.

With regard to the need to do the right thing and not the wrong thing; it is nevertheless often the case that despite every effort to do the right thing you still do the wrong thing (there are plenty of others who will deliberately, through peer pressure, or inadvertently, try to influence and mislead you, e.g. to take up an 'Us and Them' attitude by becoming a member of the local gang; or getting you to submit to and then adopt the propaganda issued by a particular ideology, cult, religion etc.).

If you do the wrong thing but then realise it, it's still OK provided you take responsibility for it; accepting the consequences that follow as a result and dealing with them as appropriate e.g., to apologise; to compensate by taking remedial action, or in more serious offences, to come clean and so serve the sentence handed down.

This acceptance of your responsibility and your accountability and then undergoing the consequences that follow, mean you continue to evolve in the right direction. Mistakes, failures and so on are as important, if not more so, than your successes and good fortune since they provide you with valuable experiences painful, unpleasant, and so on but, for that reason, memorable which advance your learning or spiritual depth a great deal. This is arguably evolution taking place in your lifetime leading you towards knowledge and the realisation of God.

The laws of nature and karma[20] apply.

If you are standing at the edge of a pond and throw a stone into the water, the consequent disturbance will cause waves and because of the ripple effect through the water your feet will eventually get wet. The interval between you throwing the stone (the cause) and your feet getting wet (the effect) may be such that you forget you threw the stone in the first place and so you don't realise the connection, nevertheless your feet are wet as the consequence of your action.

I have not made a study of karma, but this is karma in action according to my untutored, common-sense understanding. It is certainly and definitely true that what you think and do really matters: *"You've made your bed and you'll have to lie in it"*; *"...whatsoever a man soweth, that shall he also reap"* ... This particular quote is from the Bible i.e., Galatians VI, King James Version Ironically however, as far as I know, the concept of 'Karma' is not fully accepted in Christianity, but it is accepted and is an important concept, I believe, in Hinduism, Sikhism, Buddhism and Jainism. I must reiterate that I have not made a study of this subject.

The way I think about it is that; say, you desire money, and you wait, out of view in a dark isolated alleyway for someone to come along who you can hit on the head and rob; you hit the victim from behind; there is no one around; it is dark and there are, as far as you know, no witnesses. It may well be that you are convinced that you have got away with it, and you are very satisfied with how much money and valuables you were able to steal from your victim.

You feel really pleased with yourself, how clever, daring, strong and cool you are and how easy it is. It is, however, the case (despite you having no awareness of this), that all these actions you have performed, and all the sense-data associated with them have entered and been related together in your mind and so is incorporated into and becomes an integral part of your space-time reality.

This is the reality that you live within and will live within from then on (which goes forward with you as your baggage so to speak) i.e., you know, and God knows.

Even though you may never be brought to account for these actions in this phenomenal life (the crime being one of the many similar unsolved cases) and even though you may have forgotten about it. You will not get away with it. There is no hiding place, It is part of what you are, it influences your life from then on.

Later in your life there may come a time when your

conscience is awakened and the recollection of what you have done troubles you, e.g., waking you up during the night suffering from remorse, after all you may have even killed the person, you robbed.

As well as remorse you may become anxious e.g., you find out that new developments have taken place e.g., new forensic techniques such as DNA analysis. You may become aware that someone, because of having had their DNA taken for some entirely unconnected reason has now, subsequently been proved guilty of a crime carried out many years earlier. The knowledge that your DNA found at the scene is very likely on the police database can subsequently become an additional worry. Perhaps a routine search involving your DNA will flag up a 'match' linking you to the sense-data previously recorded at the scene of the crime incident in the alleyway.

It is similar also to the trap you can get into by being false, cheating and employing lies to somehow achieve an advantage or acquire something you want, or to become rich. Only later to realise that you must keep up the pretence, remember what lies you had committed so you don't give the game away and become exposed and then realise you are required to keep this up for evermore and that you have made a burden for yourself.

Life is so much simpler and free, if, as a matter of course, you don't tell lies, influenced perhaps by having honest friends or, say, through reading e.g., 'Crime and Punishment' as mentioned previously.

Considering 'karma' there are many examples where it

seems that entirely innocent and good people have been affected badly or have been killed; where it is difficult to imagine how they could have earned or deserved that fate e.g. in my example mentioned above, the ripples in the water that I caused through my action of throwing the stone not only made my feet wet (deservedly so) but it also swamped the feet of many others who were standing at the edge (undeservedly so).

Thinking about karma necessarily also raises the issue of reincarnation, personally I am comfortable with this concept, and it does account possibly for why some people are born and soon show they somehow have this amazing talent and knowledge of exactly what to do in their life e.g., like Mozart knocking it out at the age of 5 years old; carrying on as if it were from where he left off in a previous life.

However, no matter if reincarnation is, or is not, entirely true, or how interesting this maybe it is a pointless distraction, and a waste of time and energy to be getting yourself concerned with it. The actual reality is Here, Now and if you devote your energy to love of God you can fulfil the purpose of your life 'here and now' by realising that you are not the body, senses, mind, and intellect you were identified with at birth but rather that your true identity is the Atman (which is One with Brahman). Therefore, after death (the death of the body, the equipment, so to speak, that you were associated and identified with at birth) you can become free, knowing Brahman as your true identity and so remain Here, Now, never again to be reborn.

You construct your own private and subjective relationship of parts; your own representation of reality by relating the data which enters via the sense organs and which you reflect and think about with your mind; this leads you towards (or away from) unitive knowledge and experience of God, hence the importance of right action and right meditation.

Race, Skin colour, Gender, Ethnicity, Nationality, Language, Culture, Religion, Ideology, Rank, Status, Caste, Mode of dress, Length of hair, Wealth, Beauty, and all other myriad factors are utterly irrelevant to the devotee.

God is 'One'; infinite and eternal; omnipresent; the ground

and support of all space-time creation; the screen which underlies the entire space-time show equally present in all: the inanimate/animate; rich/poor; female/male; black/white; good/bad and so on.

Although the myriad factors, as listed above, are indeed irrelevant to the devotee, this assumes the devotee is a properly functioning human being with faculties intact and in good working order and so can reason, discriminate, and meditate.

There are said to be different types of human beings.

One system, by Sheldon, postulates three physical and psychological types i.e., the endomorph, mesomorph, and the ectomorph.[21]

In the Gita it describes the contemplative type who takes the path of knowledge and the active type who takes the path of selfless action.

Whichever type you happen to be whatever your natural path, you arrive at the same place, so to speak. This essay reflects my path which is predominantly that of the ectomorph and the contemplative, or Jnana yoga, type (see entry number 21 and entry number 46 in the Notes section).

You may be able to appreciate the difficulties of language; God is not **IN** space-time (in the same way that the screen is not **IN** the film show). God, the screen is invisible, formless, and non-material, without parts; it cannot (in itself) be seen or described. God, or the screen, is omnipresent so there is nowhere you can go. God, the screen is always 'Here', 'Now'.

However, in writing this I am recognising that I was born into our space-time world, identified with this body at birth and starting out life ignorant of both the relative and the absolute reality. I had first to learn about the relative reality (space-time, film show) then go on to learn about the absolute reality (God, the screen). Certainly, I did have to travel, metaphorically speaking, I did have to take appropriate action and I did have to meditate[22] and I will have to continue to do so until it is no longer necessary.

Assuming your faculties are intact, and you can reason and discriminate then the only obstacle for you to overcome is ignorance (of God's presence); however, despite being a human being and so having the means and opportunity (assuming you want to take it) there are difficulties on the way and, of course, certain preconditions have to be met.

1. You can't do anything unless you have enough to eat to sustain yourself, have access to warmth, shelter and so on. You need to work to earn the money to provide for these and to pay your bills. You need to eat to live and not live to eat (there is a profound difference).

    God (the screen) is the same to all and it is irrelevant whether you are rich or poor, however, to be poor is an advantage I believe, it might even be necessary, since being poor means you experience the raw (space-time / phenomenal) reality; you get to know the real value of things (even the value of money itself) and you can become spiritually deeper and more receptive as a result.

    Whereas to be rich often means you live in a comfortable and artificial state of reality, insulated from, or out of touch with the mundane and often unpleasant normal (space-time / phenomenal) reality. Being rich can be enjoyable, one interesting, pleasurable experience followed by another interesting, pleasurable experience and so on. There is therefore probably little motivation or desire to give up these interesting, pleasurable experiences to turn inward, looking for a deeper spiritual experience.

    The contentment and bliss you feel, say, on a warm pleasant sunny day, floating in your swimming pool mostly derives from the physical experience of the phenomenal environment itself; bolstered and enhanced, say, by the underlying security and inner contentment you feel from having money in the bank; having no debts or anything to worry about; having interesting friends and enjoying a fulfilling social and love life. You might meditate (unlikely perhaps that you would feel the need or want to do this) but then be misled, by your favourable circumstances, into assuming the bliss you experience is a sign of your success in meditation and therefore lack the determination to persist and go deeper.

If, however, for you the sun is not shining, you don't have a swimming pool or a garden or a house; you don't have money in the bank, no money spare for pleasure and leisure, feel insecure and isolated, without friends or an active love life, and so on. Then if you meditate you know that the bliss you eventually experience is 'real', a result of your meditation alone, the knowledge and experience you attain inspires you to persist and to go deeper. This changes your life e.g., you cease to feel a sense of resentment with your lot; the need or desire to have a swimming pool, garden, house etc.; the need to have a large amount of money in the bank; to have lots of friends and an active love life etc. This knowledge gives you a purpose, not any type of purpose but the 'real, true purpose' to your life and saves you from wasting all that time and effort on acquiring wealth, status, recognition and so on.

2. You need to have independence of mind; the ability to think, read, and write and the determination to take responsibility for yourself. You need the freedom to access information; generally, to facilitate your ability to earn a living but also specifically; to facilitate your spiritual progress. I believe it may be possible that you can find your way entirely through your own actions and meditation, but you will benefit very greatly from such works as 'The Bhagavad Gita' and 'The Crest Jewel of Discrimination' to name the main two texts that have aided me so much and to which I refer in this essay. You will greatly appreciate and be very grateful to those who have translated and published these works, making then affordable and easily available in a bookshop or via the Web.

3. You need to be aware that you have (to a lesser or greater degree) been conditioned, indoctrinated, socialised, and influenced by your parents, peers and so on within the society, culture, religion, and ideology etc., in which you have been born and raised.

You need to recognise this and overcome it in yourself, not by violent rebellion or political action; whatever but by being yourself, taking responsibility for your own thinking, decisions, and actions and by keeping a low profile i.e., there is no need whatsoever, to make any visible show of your holiness and your devotion – that in actual fact is your ego taking over and you don't want to give the ego any leeway or space to develop. You know and God knows – who else is there?

4. You need to exercise self-control over your desires and appetites (which may arise naturally, but which are also exacerbated and stimulated by conditions you are exposed to e.g., nature/nurture influences[23]; blood chemistry; your psychological type; peer pressures; commercial advertising pressures, drugs, and such like).

5. You need to practice and develop high moral[24] standards. This is not a matter of becoming a 'goody – goody' to impress others, to win public esteem or recognition (your objective is, after all and vitally, to overcome your ego not to develop it). Gaining control of your ego is a necessary preparation because only then can you clearly realise that 'God, Is, Here, Now'.

God is a given i.e., God is God, what you must do is to remove your ignorance, i.e., remove the mistaken identification of yourself with the body, senses, mind and intellect and the phenomenal day to day reality, then when your ego (this false identification) is sufficiently diluted, this ignorance is dissipated and God's presence is revealed, and 'union' established.

Developing high moral standards is necessary to weaken this mistaken identification. If you were fortunate enough to have had good parents, who were good role models and who instilled into you good practices e.g., from an early age; always to offer your sweets to others before taking one for yourself, and to regard others or treat others as you would like to be treated yourself. It would then, as a result, be natural for to you grow up and continue to practice these, and similar, habits into your adult life.

If you have grown up to be unselfish then you will have benefited in ways you may not realise e.g., you will have acquired a depth and a knowledge that others, who only think of their own interests, will lack. It is common sense really, I mean, if you are always straight with others and treat them as you yourself would wish to be treated, they will recognise and value you as trustworthy, straight, and true and therefore they will be much more open with you, speaking freely, giving you the benefit of their experience and so on. This increases your knowledge and understanding; whereas with others they will not recognise the same qualities as being present and they will be more closed and guarded with what they say and reveal.

Your unselfishness must have no hidden motives i.e., you give or help without expecting or wanting any recognition or reward ...

Krishna:	Krishna:
The seers say truly That he is wise Who acts without lust or scheming For the fruit of the act: His act falls from him, Its chain is broken Melted in the flame of my knowledge. Turning his face from the fruit, He needs nothing: The Atman is enough, He acts, and is beyond action, Prabhavananda and Isherwood (Page 62 - 63)	 The wise call that man wise; and such an one, Renouncing fruit of deeds, always content. Always self-satisfying, if he works, Doth nothing that shall stain his separate soul, Sir Edward Arnold (Page 45)

I am not an expert, nor do I have answers to all the problems encountered in general life e.g. I don't always give to people in the street especially if they are standing there with a bucket (if not one of the well-known 'flag day' charities).

I have always struggled with the idea of giving to people who are just begging believing sometimes that it is the wrong action to take and just encourages begging as a way of life, especially if they are young and have arms and legs like the rest of us. If I do walk by however, I feel a kind of remorse or shame; after all I have been in the position of having only loose change in my pocket and nowhere to sleep.

Eventually I realised the solution was to direct every action to God (who is equal to all) so it's not giving to the beggar so much as giving with love to God who is within the beggar. I believe also it's not the amount given that matters as much as the fact that it is given at all (with love for God). I don't mean, therefore to give only a minimum, taking the view that it's just symbolic but rather I mean to give what you can afford and what is proportionate, often this, for me, is as little as £1 or £2, (remember there is probably another beggar round the corner) and always to give in a good manner i.e. give to God, after all God is equally present within both you and the beggar and you both benefit.

Sometimes you are reluctant to give because the beggar, you imagine (possibly wrongly), is only going to 'piss' your hard earned money up against the wall or use it to buy drugs, however if this is so then so be it, he/she is responsible for his/her actions as you are responsible for yours.

Another method which I see as a solution to dealing with these issues is to give a percentage of your disposable income to charities via standing order or direct debit. I have only recently become aware however that some of the established charities, it seems, have now become political in outlook and have 'Chief Executives' and staff who get paid salaries far above the average wage and in some cases over £100,000 pa, also some of these charities have incomes from donations far greater than I ever imagined, I don't like knowing that my very limited donations over the years in effect contributed only to paying the cost of the chief executive for a day or so of his time.

On knowing this I removed all those charities from further consideration and cancelled their direct debits. I did not have any guilt about this since there are numerous charities and I could only ever support just a few therefore I decided what charities to support, excluding those who paid unreasonably large salaries to their own staff or pursued (in an undeclared manner) a political agenda or were very rich in donations anyway. I then took the mathematical approach of donating a regular percentage of about 10% of my income (after meeting unavoidable outgoings, rent, gas etc.) and making this automatic by arranging the payments through direct debit.

There is then a kind of liberation since the issue is sorted, and you can then forget about it. Freeing you thereby to devote that much more of your time and effort to establishing 'union', this is more important than anything else.

To reach union is the greatest contribution it is possible to make for the benefit of everyone on the entire planet and puts you in a position to help others e.g., when giving the £1- or £2-coin (to God who is within the beggar) God accepts it, and in a manner of speaking comes to the surface, there can be the realisation that you, the beggar and God are 'One'. This shared experience may mean the beggar undergoes a similar experience to that I referred to previously when I became aware of the seabed within me. For the first time the beggar also may become aware of it within him or herself, and so despite you not knowing (and probably never to see him or her again), your action may have started him or her onto the 'path' so to speak.

It must be remembered also that there are always disasters happening from time to time e.g., the earthquake and so on which require a response, gladly given and which reminds you (and makes you appreciate) your own comparatively good fortune.

Personally, I don't think, despite being greatly moved, that it is sensible that you should respond by selling your house, so to speak, and giving everything, you have, to relieve the suffering of others. This because through this action of compassion and generosity you will as a result impoverish yourself creating difficulties and interrupting your progress via meditation, towards union.

I think it's best to support yourself; pay your way; keep it simple; and avoid over ascetic practices. Instead to regard your body etc. as equipment which you need to maintain and treat properly, but be in control of, so you can make progress towards 'union' – in this life – with the minimum of delay.

I must mention that I don't know whether my solution is the right and proper approach, the important thing is that it is my approach and my responsibility, and I am accountable to God for my actions whether they be right or wrong.

Although it is true that you should never act with the motive to gain a reward or recognition, popularity or in any other way develop your ego. You will nevertheless often gain or be rewarded in another sense; this is unforeseen but powerful.

One experience I had occurred on a tube train, I was alone in the carriage apart from three skinhead style young men at the far end obviously going for a night out. As they got up to leave, I noticed one of them left a slim wad of money behind, it had slipped out of his back pocket, I called out to him just in time for him to realise what had happened and for him to retrieve it and then leave before the doors closed to catch up with his mates but as he did so he acknowledged his gratitude to me in a completely genuine and open manner.

Whereas, before this incident I felt a bit uncomfortable and vulnerable, a reaction to their skinhead appearance and manner, now because of his reaction I experienced and became aware that the 'Self' within him was the same 'Self' that was within me.

This was a moment of spiritual 'enlightenment' (the gain and reward I refer to above) and I realised that it was an experience that could not have been obtained in any other way, no matter how rich you might be, 'enlightenment' is an experience that cannot be bought. It is also an example of the habit of unselfishness and empathy instilled in me by my mother now, much later bearing fruit in my life and to my lasting benefit (e.g., when she taught me to share my sweets and so on when I was a young child).

This was the reason my immediate action was to call out. I was aware that I could easily have delayed my response. In a few seconds he would have left the carriage, and then all I had to do was walk down to the far end and pick up the money and add it to my wallet. No one would know (except me, and God of course). There was no way I could get the money back to the man it belonged to, indeed being at the far end I could not even identify him other than he was a young man in the dress and manner of a 'skinhead'.

Many perhaps would regard it as stupid not to have waited those few seconds it took for the man to have left the carriage. It is very easy, also to pretend to oneself that there was no time to do anything anyway and really the money has fallen into my hands like a gift from God, and the appropriate response would be to have enjoyed this good fortune which had come my way and, after all, it's not like I had stolen the money or done anything wrong.

For me to warn him was mainly an automatic, unthinking reaction but it was never a problem, and I would not have wanted to hesitate, it was a kind of victory and it sort of made my day. I appreciated having resolved it in his favour, the experience was greatly intensified for me because it so met the criteria, so to speak, of not acting to gain recognition or personal gain.

I was aware, however that my experience from childhood onwards had shown me the value of being useful in this sort of situation and that the experience undergone, and the awareness attained, so very, very, much, outweighed the monetary gain I would otherwise have obtained.

You need to develop even vision i.e., God is 'One' (although unseen) within the perceptual field just like the screen is 'One' (although unseen) within the ever-changing film-show.

As a devotee through persistence in meditation, you can become totally aware of the screen's presence and, so to speak, you can 'see' and 'hear' it, infinitely 'here', eternally 'now' even though this is apparently a nonsensical statement. The screen, to reiterate, has no parts and being beyond reach of the senses it cannot itself be seen by the eyes or heard via the ears. This is the problem with using language; it is only useful (when referring to God); to provide an analogy and act as a signpost.

The task is not easy, however don't let yourself be put off

and so not even make a start, remember you are superimposed on God therefore the resources are already within you.

You don't have to go anywhere, since God Is Infinitely Here, Eternally Now.

The Whole and the Parts

Consider a pattern defined as:

a. The Whole is within[25] each Part.
b. The Whole is greater than the sum total of Parts.
c. The Whole remains the same independently of a change in the Parts.

It is the pattern by which the Whole (God or Absolute reality) gives expression of itself through Parts (Space-time) and their evolution yet, nevertheless, remains omnipresent and distinct.

1. The Whole cannot be known and realized by investigation of the Parts.
   "He is not knowable by perception turned inwards or outwards or by both combined. He is neither that which is known, nor that which is not known nor is he the sum total of all that might be known. He cannot be seen, grasped, bargained with. He is indefinable, unthinkable, indescribable".[26]

2. The Whole can only be known and realized through union with it.
   "He is Atman, the spirit himself that cannot be seen or touched, that is above all distinction, beyond thought and ineffable. In the union with him is the supreme proof of his reality. He is the end of evolution and non-duality. He is peace and Love".

When attempting to understand the 'whole' by investigating the 'parts' we come up against an impenetrable barrier. This barrier has no real existence but rather comes into being whenever we examine symbols (representations) but then attribute to these a literal meaning.

The 'whole', therefore, which they symbolically represent, becomes disregarded or dismissed, as beyond examination, a matter of mere metaphysical speculation.

The barrier therefore is created between the 'whole' (absolute reality) on the one hand and the 'parts' (space-time or phenomenal reality) on the other.

This in effect is a relationship between 'actual experience' and the 'symbols of experience'; in other words: a relationship between 'consciousness' and the 'contents of consciousness'.

It is only possible to represent experience by using symbols. The barrier exists because we identify 'experience' with the 'symbols' themselves; because we identify 'consciousness' with the 'contents' of consciousness.

If the 'whole' (absolute reality) is identified with the 'parts' (phenomenal reality) how indeed can the 'whole' become known and realized as within the parts, beyond them and independent of them?

Consider a magnetic field we can say, the magnetic north and south poles define its limits. But to describe 'north' or even think about north in isolation to its relationship to 'south' is impossible. To say 'North' is really the same as to say, 'the opposite of South' and vice versa. The 'real' nature of North and South and the magnetic field they define is unknown and lies beyond (albeit within) the relationship.

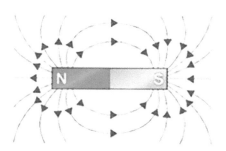

Similarly, the perceptual field has limits defined by physical-objects (bodies, trees, tables etc.) as one pole and sense-data (colour, sound, smell, texture etc.) as the other pole.

How can we describe, or even think about, a table other than to describe it's associated sense data, e.g., a table is square, brown, hard etc. or on the other hand how can we describe square, brown, hard etc. other than by pointing to a physical object which exhibits such sense-data e.g., a table.

The 'real' nature of physical-objects, sense-data, and the perceptual field so defined is unknown and lies beyond, albeit within, the relationship.

If we now consider space-time as a relationship, the limits of which are defined by 'cause' and 'effect' then we can, using these terms of reference, give a definition of:

Physical objects as:

> *The labels we give to denote definite or regularly perceived causes.*

And sense-data as:

> *The labels we give to denote the effects of these causes.*

This definition must be qualified in that:

> *It is the effects of causes, which determine our interpretation of the causes.*

Our sensation, or experience, of sense-data is private and subjective and the physical-objects are subjectively interpreted to be public and objective. The sensation or experience is the end event of a long chain of cause and effect. The sensation is completely distinct from the physical stimuli originating in the external world which excite our sensory organs.[27]

In short, whatever the reality is of physical-objects or sense data and all they define, we will never perceive it directly, this is because the sensation takes place in our brain/mind, the picture we have of the outside world is a mentally symbolic representation. Reality will not be known by examining its space-time structure.

I.e., The Whole cannot be known and realized by investigation of the Parts.

Space-time (the phenomenal universe) has no reality in itself but exists only in that middle state i.e., the perceptual field (our mentally symbolic representation of reality).

This relationship of parts (space-time) is complex, and everything is interconnected; related together by the laws of cause and effect. The 'Whole' is equally present within each part, greater than the sum of all the parts and yet remains unchanged and independent of them.

The 'Whole' is to the parts and their relationships as the 'screen' is to the 'film-show' projected upon it.

In our normal day to day life, we may be unaware and unconcerned about the reality (the Whole) which is manifested by the physical object (the relationship of parts i.e., sense-data) that we perceive.

Nonetheless we do have this awareness of 'is-ness' between the perception of one physical object and the next: between one day and the next. This is the experience of the reality (the Whole), but heavily veiled and refracted by the false identification of it with the physical object.

We have the awareness of 'is-ness' with us when we perceive, say a table, it remains with us when we next perceive a table, even though no two tables are exactly alike. There are obvious differences of size, shape, height, colour; even the *same* table is not the same. The table, being a physical object, is just a cloud of sense data and is continuously changing second by second, day by day.

Our own phenomenal body also changes second by second, day by day, for example, there isn't a single red blood cell circulating in our blood stream that is more than 120 days old. So, even the body, which we falsely identify ourselves as being, is not real, having only a transient phenomenal reality.[28]

The awareness of the 'Self' (the Whole) however still persists, and I confidently expect this awareness to remain the same even if my leg is amputated, or as I (the body that is) age, lose my teeth, my hair and so on. This 'is-ness' is independent of the relationship of parts superimposed upon it.

If we think of the perceptual field as if it were a painting. It is then like trying to know and realise the 'Whole' by investigating the painting: e.g., the paint; the brushwork; the perspective and so on. These constituent parts are analysed and broken into their own internal constituent parts.

Each of these internal parts itself is examined and often found, yet again, to have their own internal relationship of parts, then each of these internal parts themselves are found to have an internal relationship of parts, and so on.

A great deal of information is uncovered, and the complexity is such that there are different areas of investigation, undertaken by specialized teams, one studying the structure of the paint, one studying the brushwork, one the composition ... The painting itself having been dismantled, labelled, processed, and spread out among many different investigators can no longer be seen for what it is.

After each investigator has gone as far as they can in their specialised field of study, they find, despite having made remarkable progress in uncovering and understanding the space-time phenomenal structure of the painting, that they have still not made any progress in understanding the reality (the Whole).

The reason is because they have assumed the reality of the painting to be the painting itself. Not only this but crucially they assume, with understandable confidence, that they know all that can be known i.e., the painting has been shown to be, beyond dispute, **nothing but** paint, brushwork, perspective etc. and those others who speak otherwise e.g., of an 'absolute reality' being 'within but beyond' the painting are deluded.

It is possible to regard the phenomenal universe (space-time, in its entirety) to be a creation (like the painting), which manifests and gives expression to God's presence (the Whole). This can raise the idea that God is the creator, like the painter is the creator of the painting. However, God Is, Here, Now, one without a second; omnipresent, but God is never the doer, God simply Is.

In the cosmology of Shankara[29] the creator is called 'Iswara'. Iswara is Brahman/Atman[30] (God, the ultimate reality underlying all phenomena) united with 'Maya' (the play and evolution of the phenomenal universe). It is Iswara that creates, preserves, and dissolves the universe in an endless and beginning less process.

Once the parts are projected, they start participating

together according to the laws of physics e.g., responding to the force of gravity, forming many and various relationships. This process developing automatically or naturally, is evolution.

Iswara or the creator is, for me, the lack of unity in the relationships and this lack is the very force that drives the process of evolution onward and will do so unceasingly until the former unity is regained.

There are said to be six finely tuned numbers that constitute a recipe, or a set of conditions, for a space-time universe to evolve.[31] If any one of these six numbers were to be out of tune there would be no stars and no life.

The first impression, or interpretation (difficult to avoid having, considering how these numbers have to be so finely tuned) is to assume that it cannot possibly be a coincidence and there must be a creator who designed it this way.[32]

Given that God is not the 'doer', but is infinite and eternal, there is no reason why there are not an infinite number of potential universes; all those starting that don't meet the finely tuned conditions do not evolve, but eventually it comes to pass that a potential universe does indeed meet the conditions and so it evolves and hence that is why we are here now. This seems entirely possible and reminds me of the 'The Infinite Monkey Theorem' which states that a monkey hitting keys at random on a typewriter keyboard for an infinite amount of time will almost surely type a given text, such as the complete works of William Shakespeare, In fact, the monkey would almost surely type every possible finite text an infinite number of times.

What started me personally on this path, in a meaningful way, was my interest in Western science and the process of evolution.

I experienced a profound 'eureka' moment when I realised all matter is made of atoms, each[33] an interaction between three particles or force-fields: the Proton (Positive), Electron (Negative) and the Neutron (Neutral).[34]

The interactions and combinations of these three particles or forces, in my mind, can be in harmony and supportive i.e. predominantly positive – so evolving strong and enduring relationships and raising the degree of manifestation (of the Whole); or they may be in disharmony and opposing each other i.e. predominantly negative – so evolving weak and short lived relationships lowering the degree of manifestation; or they may be balanced i.e. neutral – a relationship in equilibrium (unity), neither falling back and disintegrating nor moving forward and expanding, but rather, revealing (the Whole) i.e. for that relationship it is the end of its evolution.

Later when I came across and read the Bhagavad-Gita I was very moved and satisfied that everything needed was in this work and for me there was no longer any conflict, or feelings of disloyalty to science; especially when I went on to read about the description of Maya as the interplay and evolution of three Gunas i.e., Rajas (Kinesis), Tamas (Inertia) and Sattwa (Illumination). For me Rajas equated, as a way of thinking, to the (positive) proton, Tamas to the (negative) electron, and Sattwa to the (neutral) neutron.[35]

The Book as a Creation

If we consider an individual who has, say through his own actions, reasoning, and meditation undergone a revelatory experience of the 'Whole', then this experience is subjective and private to him or her alone.

The individual let us say an author, if he/she wants to tell others the good news realises that this is not possible (no one can experience this reality which is subjective and private to him/her alone).

The most suitable action for him/her perhaps, is to write a book i.e., to create a relationship of parts (letters), which will explain, represent, or at least vouch that this experience truly exists and can be experienced and entered into if the appropriate action and meditation is carried out.

The book when created and published is then in the public domain, a physical object in the perceptual field. Other individuals provided they can see, read, and understand the language in which the book is written, have the opportunity to obtain this book and by reading it transfer the sense-data (the public parts which construct the book) via their sensory organs and nervous system into their brain[36] where, subjectively, and privately, they can reconstruct the relationship created by the author.

The reader may be inspired by the author's evidence and his testimony, and so carry out the necessary activities described. The authors intention and hope of course is that the reader will then undergo that same experience and so attain to 'union'.

The experience (the 'Whole') is the same and independent of the parts and their relationship, the book for example can be written in any language, It is not the case that since one has learnt one language from the many existing, that the experience can only be experienced in that one language. It is the languages that are many and different not the experience.

The author's medium is 'language' which consists of

'Words', which themselves consist of 'Letters'. The author therefore has available, using the English language, 26 parts,[37] – the **Letters** of the alphabet.

The letters in themselves are meaningless but the author selects and relates different groups of them to form **Words.** The words range from the simple at one end of the scale to complex at the other. Each Word is a manifestation of the Whole. It is a question of degree, not of a difference in kind, i.e., it is always the same experience (Whole) but the degree to which this is manifested varies with each word.

The Word is a relationship of parts, but each Word now becomes itself, a part and is employed in the next development of the book. The author working with these Word-parts creates new relationships, to form **Sentences**. As with words each Sentence manifests the whole according to the simplicity or complexity of its structure.

The next stage of development makes use of these Sentences, as Parts, to relate them together to form **Paragraphs.**

Many Paragraphs: each having its own history of development then are related together with other Paragraphs as the Parts which form a **Chapter.**

The **Book** is completed when these Chapters, as Parts, are brought together into a final relationship.

The Book is a manifestation created by the author, of the private and subjective experience (the 'Whole'). The manifestation is a concrete form, public and objective.

If you examine the Book, you find it contains nothing but letters. The 26 types of letters are meaningless and manifest nothing in themselves. The 'Whole' is within each letter, greater than the sum total of letters and independent of them.

The book is a construction, which serves the purposes of communication; it exists within the perceptual field, public and objective. It is like a bridge where we can, through reading, cross over from the public and objective into the private and subjective. The reader when reading the book goes through the same process of creation and so deepens and expands the experience of the whole, which each successive relationship serves to manifest.

Communication is perfect when the relationships created in the mind of the reader correspond to those created in the mind of the author and so the reader experiences union (oneness) with it.

The author

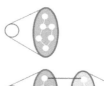

An experience is undergone, and the author gives manifestation to this experience by creating a relationship of parts.

If the same relationship of parts which gives manifestation to this experience is created in the mind of the reader, then the experience is undergone through union.

The Creation as a Book

If you consider the creation and evolution of the phenomenal (space-time) universe you can see the same pattern:

Whole → Parts → Whole.

It is the pattern by which the Whole (God or Absolute reality) gives expression of itself through 'Parts' and their evolving relationships (phenomena or space-time) yet, nevertheless, remains omnipresent and distinct.

Instead of the 26 parts i.e., letters, which make up the English language, we need only to consider the 3 particles which make up the physical matter of the universe i.e., the Proton, Neutron, and the Electron.[38]

The common atomic model I grew up with consisted of a nucleus (of protons and neutrons) surrounded by orbiting electrons. This is however a mental manifestation created by human beings e.g., the electron is said not to truly exist in space-time but only emerges into momentary actual existence through the act of measurement.[39]

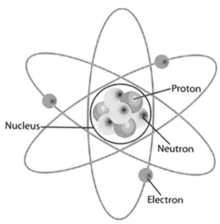

The parts (both 'letters' and 'particles') and their evolving relationships are illustrated in the diagram on the next page:

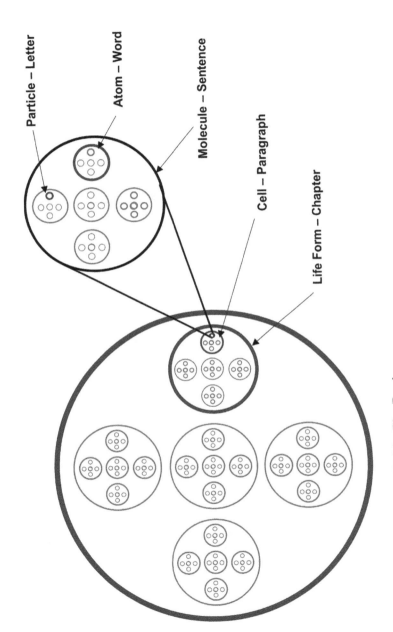

Particle – Letter

Atom – Word

Molecule – Sentence

Cell – Paragraph

Life Form – Chapter

The Created Field – The Book

A 'circle' is an imaginary boundary used here only to give us a way of visualising the process, so to start:

A 'circle' represents the Letter (or the Particle).

The Word (Atom) is represented by a 'circle' which encompasses its internal relationship of Letters (or Particles).

The Sentence (or Molecule) is represented by a 'circle' which encompasses its internal relationship of Words (or Atoms).

The Paragraph (or Cell) is represented by a circle which encompasses its internal relationship of Sentences (or Molecules).

The Chapter (or Life-form) is a circle which encompasses its internal relationship of Paragraphs (or Cells).

Finally (for our purposes) the evolved end product is the 'Book (an internal relationship of 'Chapters') or the Human being (the most evolved life-form)

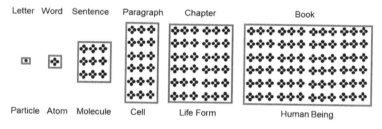

Letter   Word   Sentence   Paragraph   Chapter   Book

Particle   Atom   Molecule   Cell   Life Form   Human Being

This simplified diagram is meant to show that at the fundamental level the book (or the created field) consists of nothing but letters (or particles).

Because the reality (Whole) remains the same independently of a change in the parts we can compare the book with the phenomenal universe.

In the same way we talked about the creation of the book from the letters to the word, the words to the sentence then the sentences to the paragraph, the paragraphs to the chapter and finally the chapters to the book.

We can talk about the creation (evolution) of phenomena as being the particles relating together to form the atom, the atoms to form the molecule, the molecules to form the cell and the cells to form the life-forms, the most evolved of which being the human being.

Consider that the book, on examination, consists only of

letters. Now, consider and examine the human-being, each and every one (also each and every other life form) and indeed all space-time phenomena, throughout the entire universe, actually consists of nothing but 'particles'

Remove the imaginary boundaries (circles) in the diagrams and the page loses its form i.e., becomes blank, or out of focus. Remember as previously mentioned an electron particle is said not to truly exist in space and time but only emerges into momentary actual existence through the act of measurement (presumably this may be true for all particles?). I have not made a study of Bishop Berkley's philosophy of immaterialism and perhaps I am being very frivolous, but it seems to me that to say 'by the act of measurement' is similar to saying 'by the act of perception').

If we become concerned about the 'absolute reality' and now regard it as being the omnipresent and distinct 'Whole' (i.e., 'Screen') pervading the perceived object e.g., the 'table' or the 'human being' or any other physical object or phenomena then we are, as it were, 'reading' the book i.e., aligning the relationship of parts with the purpose of realizing that which they serve to manifest.

I must point out that this is just my way of looking at things, I am not a scientist or philosopher, I have however been heavily influenced by widespread reading and in particular, the section concerning 'orthogenesis'[40] as described by 'Teilhard de Chardin' in his work "The Phenomenon of Man".

I accept that I have probably not done justice to this work and my use of the words 'Within' and 'Without' is my interpretation and does not equate exactly with the usage of these words by Teilhard de Chardin.

My view then is that the 'Whole' IS and that it requires manifestation of itself, this process is initiated by projecting a variety of 'parts', which, through evolutionary activity, enter into myriad relationships, these relationships serve to give manifestation and expression to the 'Whole'.

The eternally changing 'Many' is superimposed upon the eternally unchanging 'One'.

i.e., the relative or phenomenal reality is superimposed upon the Absolute reality, which is to say, the contents of consciousness are superimposed upon consciousness.

It is a question of there being a false or true identification i.e., that which is united with the Whole through previous creations remains united and that which has not; becomes identified with the parts and their relationships and so again enters the relationship i.e., is born.

The Whole is identified to the parts and remains so only until it is realised as distinct from them.

Two terms: the 'within' and the 'without' are used frequently in the following account. The term 'within' represents the 'Whole', the 'screen', Brahman, Atman, the Self, Absolute Reality, pure consciousness, or the 'existent' (i.e., all the terms used to mean God)' but the 'within' differs because it is Brahman identified with the parts and their relationships (i.e., referred to as the Atman) and so appears to be confined inside them, separate and therefore is born.

The term 'without' represents the environment, the body and all the parts and their relationships as seen from the viewpoint of the 'within'.

The starting point is the state of equilibrium; the relationship of parts is balanced; at rest; space-time is not manifest; the film-show has not started; the screen alone IS,

This state of equilibrium is then disturbed e.g., say, 'Big Bang', this results in the state of unity becoming fragmented and the parts projected. As a simplification let's say of 3 types e.g., Neutron (Neutral),[41] Proton (Positive) and Electron (Negative) these combine together into various relationships i.e., Atoms, initially Hydrogen and Helium, the other atoms and elements being created later.[42]

The Atoms fall into what may be described as an atomic orthogenesis, the simplest, say the hydrogen atom, at one end and the most complex, say uranium, at the other.

The atoms (now Parts) interact with each other in various ways giving rise to molecules; similarly, there is a molecule orthogenesis from micro-molecules to mega-molecules.

This primary stage concerns the evolution of inanimate matter. The minerals and so on are perfected in that no further improvement is possible; such matter remains stable because of its rigid internal structure, consequently the 'within' is entombed.

The most complex of mega-molecules reaches a stage of development whereby it's 'within' becomes critical i.e., reaching a point of transition from one state to another. The motivation, which inspires or drives evolution, is towards regaining balance or equilibrium in the relationship; therefore, they develop, expand, acquire new parts, and vary their internal relationship.

In the highest development of mega-molecules, this motivation is still present, so further development is required. It is possible that the inanimate becomes animate when two mega-molecules both with a critical 'within' combine into one relationship, releasing life-energy to form a new relationship i.e., the cell (the living part).

The cell with its life inspired 'within' grows by assimilating and consuming it's 'without'. As a consequence, the cell divides and duplicates itself. The birth rate of cells continues according to geometric progression and the cells multiply to an extent (due to the finite surface of the earth) whereby the shortage of living space forces the cells to go through an inner readjustment. This results in the cells taking on new appearance and direction and causes uniformity to give way to diversification.

This stage gives rise to sexual reproduction, a mechanism of evolution, which results in endless permutations and character combinations i.e., genetics.

The outcome to multiplication and diversification of living matter is association. In this, cells congregate into various relationships and thus become a greater manifestation of the 'Whole'. This gives rise to an orthogenesis.

The simpler life relationships are aggregates as in bacteria and the lower kinds of fungi. Higher life forms are the colony of attached cells, as seen in vegetable forms and the lower classes of molluscs. More complex still is the cell of cells as in metazoan and other animal forms.

Through multiplication, diversification, and association there is evolution from the simple to the complex, from seaweed and sponges to fish, and then to land plants, amphibians, insects and reptiles, mammals, birds, primates, and human beings.

The success of this progress depends on the ability to pass on information from one generation to the next, by way of genes and heredity.

In the contest between the ever-expanding masses of life forms there arises the principle of survival of the fittest by natural selection. This operates by favouring the reproduction of certain life forms more than that of others, the effect of this being to bring about alterations in the store of genes as they pass from one generation to the next. Another factor is the capacity of the individual life form to select out of the range open to them, the particular environment in which they pass their life and therefore to influence the type of natural selection to which they will be subjected.

In this fashion life forms advance along their particular pathways, the 'within' draws in and assimilates the 'without' and so becomes ever more complex, integrated, and conscious.

Many life forms eventually reach a state of perfected adaptation to their respective environments becoming, so to speak, precision tools for survival.

When the stage whereby no further improvement is possible the 'within' is entombed and the life form reproduces itself according to its evolved i.e., settled (apart from the possibility of mutation) genetic blueprint.

In the higher life forms, the complexity of the developing relationship is such that in order for the 'within' to deal with and assimilate the 'without' a brain served by a nervous system and sensory organs has evolved.

This mechanism reaches a critical stage in the development of the super-animal, super-animal becomes pre-man because it is still imperfectly related to the 'without' but able to walk, thus allowing the hands to be free. The ability to manipulate the 'without', using the hands and objects as tools brings about further development of the brain and nervous system. Eventually a point is reached when the 'within' becomes so conscious as to become conscious of itself (as the 'within').

This is the turning point or threshold, and it is consciousness of the 'within' as being the 'self', that differentiates the human being from other life forms.

A new mechanism becomes available for the transmission of information from one generation to the next this being communication and education.

Mankind multiplied and diversified, forming relationships, which may be described as social forms (e.g., the family, the super family, settlement, tribe, and society).

The social forms developed by drawing in and assimilating the 'without'. The 'within' of the social form might be called social consciousness. There is a social orthogenesis from the uniform society to the most complex the pluralistic society.

This section above rests very heavily on reading "The Phenomenon of Man" by 'Pierre Teilhard de Chardin' many years ago. Whether or not it suffers from my interpretation or has been superseded by more recent research doesn't concern me that much. I personally found it very helpful because, as I have already mentioned, it illustrates the underlying pattern:

Whole > Parts > Whole.

In all created forms, inanimate and animate the 'within' is conscious, but the degree of consciousness is defined and limited by the parts and their relationship.

Minerals, metals, fish, dogs, and monkeys each give manifestation to the whole.

In the case of minerals and metals this is rigid and stable, giving but a dim reflection of consciousness, vegetation expresses consciousness to a greater degree than soil, dogs more so than goldfish.

Monkeys and apes are so developed as to appear almost human; hardly surprising since they are so close to us in the evolutionary chain. That we can so easily see our human traits and characteristics manifested in the apes is because they actually are our traits and characteristics.

It is the same 'whole' but expressed by that relationship of parts; that life-form we name as the ape. The relationship of parts that results in the life-form we name as the 'human being' is more developed and so gives greater expression to that same 'whole'.

The monkeys and apes have adapted to a specific environment, a tree life secure and free from dangers present on the ground, having great freedom of movement in and about trees with access to freely available food. The 'within' is relatively content, the relationship of parts is in a reasonable state of equilibrium, therefore the motivation, the demand or necessity for further development is not there. By remaining where they are, however, they become confined to their environment so therefore it is not possible for the monkey or ape to become conscious of what lies beyond their environment. This is what is meant when describing the 'within' as being entombed.

The relationship of parts demanded by the 'whole', as it were, to proceed beyond all environments so far encountered in the created field, has evolved (in the physical or biological sense) but not yet, I believe, fully evolved in the psychological, intellectual, and spiritual sense.

The 'without' of the monkey or ape is the tree environment; for the fish it is the sea; for the bird it is the sky. The 'without' of the human being however is the entire created field i.e., the world/universe environment.

The 'within', has experienced every created relationship from the inside, so to speak, and eventually attained to human birth.

The 'within' has, so to speak, climbed to the top of the evolutionary tree then turned back on itself and realised that it IS ('I am', or more accurately, that there is an existent;).

The Turning Point

Every human being knows this 'I am' but I don't think many have realised the significance of what this really means. This is so only because they have not yet overcome their identification of the 'within' with the parts, i.e., the body, senses, mind, and intellect.

We are identified, of necessity, at birth and everything in the 'without' seems to confirm and reinforce this 'self' as we grow up, subject to this influence and that, and developed through education, socialisation and so forth.

This identification of the 'within' or 'self' to the body, senses, mind, and intellect (obviously necessary for life in the world) is yet nevertheless false.

Now that the 'Turning point' has been reached, the evolutionary way forward for the 'within' or 'self' is to overcome this false identification.

Look up now and imagine a circular boundary line framing your perceptual field, for example say you are sitting at the kitchen table, then whatever it is that you see and hear e.g., the sink, the kettle, the window (and what can be seen/heard through it), the cat, the radio and the music radiating from it and so on, know that it is just a complex relationship of parts within this imagined boundary.

You can zoom in or focus on one of the constituent parts, say the kettle, and this seems to be a separate, self-contained physical object (itself and inwardly however, having its own complex relationship of parts) occupying a specific place in the room.

The music however radiating from the radio doesn't itself seem to have a place, but rather fills your perceptual field.

Now get up and move into the garden. The parts and their relationships undergo change; the relationships within the kitchen are now behind you and beyond the boundary of your perceptual field (apart from the music, which you can still hear).

Inside this circular boundary framing the new relationship

of parts, it seems, as before, that each part in this new relationship is different and separated from every other part e.g., the sun, clouds, the garden shed, the flowerbeds, the lawn etc. The sound of traffic and garden birds may now be heard adding to the sounds of music from the radio. These sounds, although originating from different places and heard variably more strongly in one ear rather than the other depending on your movements, nevertheless fill your perceptual field.

However, although you may have settled down and are now sitting motionless in the garden deck chair; the changes nevertheless continue e.g., a cloud passes over the sun and so brings about a change of light, colour, shade, temperature and so on. The Cat runs out of the kitchen and jumps up onto the fence, the birds immediately take off and disappear into the bushes and so the changes continue onward ceaselessly.

Remember also, that the body, sensory organs, mind, and intellect, which you normally identify as your 'self', is actually itself a relationship of parts and an integral part of this perceptual field.

You feel cold, and perhaps even a little depressed because black clouds pass in front of the sun and there is a drop in temperature, the breeze may fall away, and you just know you must get up and move back into the kitchen because it is going to rain.

Realize that this identification of the 'self', with the body, sensory organs, mind, and intellect and with your local perceptual field i.e., the garden environment, and also with your wider perceptual field i.e., what is over the garden fence e.g., the neighbourhood, town, county, country, and everything else related e.g., your language, religion, culture and so on is a false identification.

Although you have grown up with this identification, it is actually false. Think of your 'self' as the 'screen' and the perceptual field, all of it (as mentioned above) as the film show projected onto it.

Recall the film-show is projected onto the 'screen' but the 'screen' is not IN the projected film-show. The 'screen' is distinct from the film-show although it pervades every part of it.

The screen is entirely itself; film-shows come and go but the screen is ever the screen.

The screen is the 'Whole' – as mentioned previously:

The Whole is within each Part.
The Whole is greater than the sum total of Parts.
The Whole remains the same independently of a change in the Parts.[43]

You might also alternatively think of the 'Whole', the true 'Self' as being like the glass mirror, it is glass throughout and doesn't ever cease to be glass.

Everything perceived is just reflections within the glass but only the glass itself is real.

Just as the 'screen' is not **IN** the film-show so the 'glass' is not **IN** these reflections.

Better still think of the 'Whole' or 'Self' as being consciousness, pure consciousness, consciousness itself and think of the perceptual field as being the 'contents of consciousness'.

If this perceptual field were a painting, you would not realize the 'Whole', the reality underlying it, by examining the paint, brushwork or other elements involved in its creation, this because you would naturally see the painting to be a 'symbolic representation'; a 'manifestation' of the reality, not the reality itself.

In fact, you would take the opposite direction, as it were, and back away to get it fully in view including its frame since this defines its limits. You would then contemplate it and meditate upon it trying to understand and become aware of the reality it manifests and is serving to communicate.

The painter (or God), as it were, has an experience; he cannot give this experience (private and subjective to him) to anyone else other than by providing a creation i.e., the painting (the perceptual field; the parts and their relationships i.e., space-time).

Unlike the case with the painting, it is not possible for you to back away since you cannot step out of space-time (i.e., go beyond the polar opposites which are its frame so to speak).

You can imagine a circular boundary line however framing your perceptual field and then contemplate and meditate on the reality this bounded view (of the perceptual field) serves to manifest.

The parts and their relationships (within this bounded view of the perceptual field) are just what they are, where they are. Everything perceived, including the stars and galaxies seen and unseen within this view cannot be anywhere but where they are, if they were any nearer, or any further away, then you would not be here to see them.

Recall that these parts and their relationships only emerge into existence by the act of perception. The stars and the galaxies are not separate and are not themselves conscious, they are, as with everything else, superimposed on the 'one' undifferentiated, omnipresent consciousness; they exist in your perceptual field because you are conscious, and you perceive them.

Whenever I read the views of some who point out how insignificant we human beings are on our insignificant planet, a tiny speck of dust located in an obscure location out in the remote backwater of a rather ordinary galaxy,

I am reminded of the fact that it is only we, evolved human beings, who are sufficiently developed and conscious enough to make these perceptions and really our decision, on the basis of our observations and our thinking, if it is to conclude that we are insignificant is to miss the point in a very big way.

If we look up or out, it is easy to be overcome by the unimaginable immensity of it all.

Within the galaxy where we are located there are about *100 billion* stars* (roughly the number of grains in a cubic metre of sand); our galaxy is nothing special being a member of a local group of about *30* galaxies*; our local group is itself nothing special since I've read that there are multiple groups of galaxies scattered, like a web, throughout the universe, in total about *100 billion* galaxies* and so on and this, remember, is just in that portion of the universe we are capable of observing at the present time; and then again our universe is now increasingly being suggested as possibly just one universe among many (the multiverse).

The numbers stated here are now out of date, currently (2023) In our galaxy there could be 1 trillion stars and in our local group there could be more than 50 galaxies (i.e., those galaxies located within 5 million light years of space around us; the diameter of our local group is about 10 million light years [a light year is the distance light travels in one year, in one second this is 186,000 miles or 300,000,000 metres, so in 1 year is 5.88 trillion miles or 9.46 trillion kilometres]). Throughout the observable universe there could be, it is estimated, 2 trillion galaxies, 1 trillion is a million million (1,000,000,000,000 or 10^{12}).

This relationship of parts is unimaginably immense (a sphere of radius 93 billion light years) and unimaginably old (13.7 billion years), but this set of relationships has evolved (deliberately or spontaneously but certainly as a prerequisite) to bring into being living creatures and us human beings.

To quote from a recent publication seen:

"Despite the vastness of the Universe, one need not feel insignificant. A diagram of mass against complexity shows that living things are enormously more complex than astronomical objects. To illustrate: If things shone with a brightness in proportion to their complexity, then galaxies would be dim light bulbs, while your brain alone would be a beacon visible across the whole universe! So, we are special, cosmically speaking."

Professor Mark Whittle

University of Virginia author/presenter of a commercially available course i.e., "Cosmology: The History and Nature of Our Universe"

Think of the Whole, as the screen and think of space-time as a film show projected upon it. Identify the Self, i.e., yourself (the capital 'S' Self)[44] with the screen and so 'One' with the 'Whole' – the eternal witness.

Discriminate between the Self (screen) and space-time (the film show).

The Whole, the Existent, Within, Self, God, Brahman, Atman, Consciousness, the Screen (apologies for using various terms for the same purpose) is the:

'ONE' – the **infinite** and eternally **unchanging absolute** reality.

The Perceptual Field; the Contents of consciousness; the Phenomenal; the Parts; the Sense data; the Without, the Film Show (again various terms for the same purpose) is the:

'MANY' – the **finite** and eternally **changing relative** reality.

The **ONE** is in the **MANY**; The **MANY** is in the **ONE**

To see the **One in the Many** and the **Many in the One** is
UNION.

His heart is with Brahman,
His eye in all things
Sees only Brahman
Equally present,
Knows his own Atman
In every creature, and all creation
Within that Atman.

That yogi sees me in all things,
and all things within me. He never
loses sight of me, nor I of him. He
is established in union with me
and worships me devoutly in all
beings. That yogi abides in me,
no matter what his mode of life.

Who burns with the bliss
And suffers the sorrow
Of every creature
Within his own heart,
Making his own
Each bliss and each sorrow;
Him I hold highest Of all the yogis.

Prabhavananda and Isherwood
(Page 84)

Of unity with Brahma. He so vowed,
So blended, sees the Life-Soul resident
In all things living, and all living things
In that Life-Soul contained. And whoso thus
Discerneth Me in all, and all in Me,
I never let him go; nor looseneth he
Hold upon Me; but dwell he where he may,
Whate'er his life, in Me he dwells and lives,
Because he knows and worships Me,
Who dwell in all which lives,
and cleaves to Me in all.
Arjuna! If a man sees everywhere –
Taught by his own similitude – one Life,
One Essence in the Evil and the Good,
Hold him a Yogi, yea! Well-perfected!

Sir Edward Arnold (Page 64)

Yoga and Meditation

The term 'yogi', also the term 'meditate' used to intimidate me and put me off. The image I had of a yogi seemed to cut me firmly out of the picture, being western, working class, lacking in physical confidence etc. As regards medi-

tation there was no way I would hitch-hike to the Himalayas and sit at the feet of a Guru, nor could I sit in the lotus position like shown. I feel inadequate and not suited to this kind of lifestyle. In the Gita there is a description on how to meditate.

The place where he sits should be firm, neither too high nor too low, and situated in a clean spot. He should first cover it with sacred grass, then with a deerskin; then lay a cloth over these. As he sits there, he is to hold the senses and imagination in check, and keep the mind concentrated upon its object. If he practises meditation in this manner, his heart will become pure. His posture will be motionless, with the body, head and neck held erect, and the vision indrawn, as if gazing at the tip of the nose. He must not look about him.

So, with heart serene & fearless,
Firm in the vow of renunciation,
Holding the mind from its restless roaming, now let him struggle to reach my oneness,
Ever absorbed, his eye on me always,
His prize, his purpose.

If a yogi has perfect control over his mind, and struggles continually in this way to unite himself with Brahman, he will come at last to the crowning peace of Nirvana, the peace that is in me.

Prabhavananda and Isherwood (Page 81/82)

In a fair, still spot
Having his fixed abode – not too much raised, nor yet too low – let him abide.
His goods a cloth, a deerskin,
and the Kusa-grass,
There, setting hard his mind upon the One,
Restraining heart and senses, silent, calm,
Let him accomplish Yoga, and achieve Pureness of soul, holding immovable Body and neck and head, his gaze absorbed upon his nose-end,
rapt from all around,
Tranquil in spirit, free of fear, intent Upon his Brahmacharya vow, devout,
Musing on Me, lost in the thought of Me.
That Yogin, so devoted, so controlled,
Comes to the peace beyond –
My peace, the peace Of high Nirvana!

Sir Edward Arnold (Page 61/62)

One thing to bear in mind, is that common sense applies e.g. the advice to first cover the seat with sacred grass, then with a deerskin etc. is traditional for that time i.e. approx. 2,500 years ago (I believe rituals are of great importance to many people but for many others e.g. like myself they have no real significance, this because I relate to Brahman as being the 'screen' and 'Here, Now', sacredness therefore is 'within' everything, *"Brahman is greater than the greatest, lesser than the least")*[45] So just find a quiet, private, comfortable spot.

For myself, however I did not take to this practice and found myself not able, or naturally suited, to meditate in this manner. I know, from my experience, that the Gita is true, so have no doubts that by following the advice for indrawn meditation, as described, that enlightenment and liberation would be achieved and I expect much more quickly than by following the path I adopted, which is, perhaps, the 'long way round'.

My meditation has been conducted with eyes open and mainly while walking the streets, sitting in the café etc. (except where music and sound is concerned e.g., at a concert or at home listening to the Hi Fi or radio).

However, though my meditation is not indrawn, I follow the advice of keeping the body, head and neck erect e.g., when sitting in the café or the park when resting from walking (it is quite natural and no one would know I was meditating) or when, at a music concert, again it is natural to sit towards the edge of the seat so that the body, head, and neck are naturally erect. This aids concentration and, though it's hard work, I follow every note of the music.

It's much easier to keep the eyes closed, so avoiding distractions and allowing one to focus solely on the music, later of course you want to have the eyes open, then it is easier at first to focus on one element only e.g., the singer: the violinist, the conductor or whoever, then you follow every movement in addition to following every note.

Later you expand the area of concentration and focus. As previously mentioned, the 'within' is always tending to expand the boundaries of the 'without', thereby increasing the amount available for assimilation.

I found going to music concerts for this purpose (especially

'Early music' or music from the 'Baroque' era), to be especially conducive to meditation – a fast track to God. This may be true but technically if you are sitting in the park listening to the sounds of traffic or to workmen drilling the road to repair a pothole it is exactly the same process – everything is superimposed on God.

I would also mention that this activity e.g. meditating following every note and movement and so on, requires concentration, and energy and you can feel the effects the next day, for me no matter how much I loved the music and no matter the joy of realisation when the music takes you into the 'screen' I had to pace myself and not, in my enthusiasm, book a place at concerts held on subsequent days e.g. pre booking to attend the regular 'Festival of Baroque' music held in London each May.

I would naturally want to do this not only because I love the music, but also because booking multiple concerts gained a significantly discounted price, I had to learn to go to just one or two rather than to each one, this might be different for someone who is younger and fitter than me.

Meditation means for me, to focus one's mind and to follow closely the sounds and sights in the perceptual field; with the aim to achieve synchronisation and so experience the Whole (or, using any of the other terms which mean the same thing, e.g., the Self (Capital S), God, Brahman, Atman, Absolute Reality, Consciousness, the Screen).

A 'yogi' means for me, any person who practices yoga i.e., union with the Whole (or as above re other terms used). The term Yoga (previously used to conjure up in my mind the picture of a 'sadhu', long hair, marked with white ash, dressed in a lion cloth ...) can mean many things as advocated by fitness trainers or spiritual gurus concerning specific bodily postures, exercises, breath control etc.

Hindu religious literature recognizes four main types of yoga (four paths to union to suit the different types of individuals) these are Karma yoga, Bhakti yoga, Jnana yoga and Raja yoga.[46]

My path, according to this categorisation is predominantly Jnana yoga, however, always remember it is a blend of all as each type of individual is a blend of the three gunas, you follow your natural predominance i.e., be yourself and remember all roads lead to the same realisation.

There is no longer, for me, anything intimidating or esoteric about the terms meditation and yoga, however, being western I still feel it is pretentious to call myself a yogi, even though I am, I have not yet talked to anyone about this but if I were to do so I would instead call myself a 'devotee'. I actually don't know how this is pronounced but whether it is 'dev'otee or 'dee'votee I know for sure that I am one and that's all that matters.

By being a devotee I mean to love God with all your heart and all your mind, this is for ever, if you have love of love, consciousness of consciousness then it is union and nothing then is going to break or obscure it; ignorance when dispelled ceases to exist; the 'I' (phenomenal self) ceases to exist (not quite true since you still have a name, pay the bills, and live normally in conventional society however the identification of the Self with the body, senses, mind or intellect ceases to exist even though the body lives on).

It is easier and helpful, I think, to start off by practicing meditation on sound, especially music. Ensure you are comfortable, not in pain, not hot or cold, not having pressing matters on your mind to disturb and distract you, now close your eyes and then the only sense data you have to deal with is the music.

Assuming the radio is switched off here in the room or garden and all is quiet, there is nevertheless music playing even though you do not know or hear it.

In fact, in my room at the moment I know by running the setup on my digital TV that there are, currently, *76* digital TV stations* and *23* digital radio stations* available to watch or listen to (also, I assume, many other e.g., those operating on different wavelengths such as the police, ambulance, coastguard, military etc.).

---

* These numbers are also now out of date, and they have increased e.g., there are now (2023) over 100 digital stations available and no doubt these numbers will continue to increase, as will the number of stars as the diameter of the observable universe continues to increase, however they are just illustrations.

The proof that this music exists is found in the experience of it and switching the radio on, then tuning to the desired programme frequency will give you this experience.

The reason I can experience the music here, now in my room, even though the musicians are playing in a studio many miles away, is because the music played in the studio is picked up by a microphone, this contains a diaphragm which vibrates in sync with the vibrations travelling through the air produced by the musicians and their instruments.

Carbon granules in the microphone[47] are compressed by the diaphragm to create electrical signals, these signals are sent to the radio transmitter, where they are superimposed onto a carrier frequency (in the radio range of the electro-magnetic radiation spectrum, say 94.9 MHz[48] assuming for our purposes this is BBC London).

This carrier frequency, so modulated,[49] is transmitted in a wave like pattern to all parts of the country; If you have a radio receiver you tune it to BBC London, which is 94.9 MHz. Tuning in causes this carrier frequency to be demodulated,[50] downloading the original superimposed electrical signals so they can be sent to the loud speaker, the vibrations of the speaker diaphragm vibrate the air; the vibrations of the air spread through the room and enter the ear to vibrate the tympanic membrane (ear drum); this vibrating membrane in turn vibrates the small ossicle bones in the inner ear which then generate fluid waves and stimulate hair cells in the cochlear, these stimulations generate electrical signals (the neurological equivalent, as it were in my imagination, of the binary 1's and 0's used in computer code) which then pass along the cochlear nerve to the area in the brain specialised for hearing.

This is a simplified layman's explanation, but it illustrates the sequence of the many cause and effect actions involved; not only is nature's physiology and brain activity very impressive but even more impressive, and a complete mystery, at least to me, is the fact that when these vibrations eventually pass into the relevant area of your brain you undergo the conscious experience of music. Such music sometimes so emotionally moving that it brings tears to the eyes. The interface between the relationships of parts and the whole i.e., how these vibrations or musical notes (contents of consciousness) give rise to the experience of music (in consciousness) is the mystery.

The sought for 'Theory of Everything'[51] (TOE) is for ever out of reach, because of that unknown and unknowable interface.

Scientists think they can pick up the story of space-time events that took place within 1 trillionth of a trillionth of a second after the 'Big Bang' event,[52] but there is no way to go beyond or before 'Big Bang' itself, for no other reason perhaps that space-time will then no longer exist and the concept of being 'beyond' or 'before' is meaningless.

It is the same issue I think when you consider anything that takes place in the perceptual field e.g., the singer in the band creates or sings the song by taking air into the lungs then passing this air out through the vocal cords.

I imagine the shaping of the oral cavity, tongue, and throat (and thus the volume) and the length and movement of the vocal folds or cords causes the molecules of air to vibrate in specific ways which radiate outwards until they reach and then vibrate the diaphragm in the microphone accordingly and so it proceeds, as previously described, until at the receiving end the vibrations of air, a faithful reproduction of those produced by the singer, enters the ear of the listener.

Before the song comes into existence i.e., before the singer starts the song there must be some kind of exercise of the will which initiates neural activity to start the process off by sending electrical signals to the centres which control breathing; which alter the shape of the oral cavity; the movements of the vocal cords and so on.

The mystery for me is what happens right at the very start how does consciousness (the Whole, which does nothing, has no parts, which simply Is, Here, Now) start the singing and musical activity going? (in space-time).

All this detail and description is only necessary perhaps to make you, the potential devotee, take God (or whatever term you prefer to use) seriously.

It is knowledge of God that you need to acquire, not necessarily knowledge of how a microphone works, how the carrier frequency is modulated and broadcasted etc. It is important, however, that the knowledge is based on logical, intelligent understanding and experience rather than just a non-thinking belief alone e.g., you are told that God is because it says so in this book, say, the Bible, the Quran, or the other scriptures.

Many have been taught that God is 'such and such' at an early age, and often before their brain has fully developed, in fact the brain, because of this early indoctrination, may well have become modelled and conditioned by this input so that afterwards, and perhaps throughout that person's life, he or she no longer has the capability of questioning and effectively their mind is closed, (the 'within' entombed). As a consequence, they are not open to reason or to anything that does not fit the mould they have been set into.

To become a devotee the person must break this mould, open the mind, and take responsibility for their own thinking, actions and meditation and so come to know God, individually, for themselves, by themselves, through union. Belief alone is very probably not adequate or sufficient.

You must experience God i.e. through union and do this while you live, after death there is no longer the opportunity since the equipment, having been cremated or buried, is not available and further progress is not possible, until, (assuming reincarnation operates) you obtain a new birth in favourable or appropriate circumstances to help and enable you to carry on, as it were, from where you left off and so make further progress leading possibly (perhaps even after many lifetimes) to attaining union and liberation.

The issue concerning the appearance of the song in the perceptual field right at the start is the same issue for the devotee who perceives the song right at the end.

The devotee, eyes closed, meditating on the vibrations (song or music) entering the ear is focused on each note of the music and the voice of the singer i.e., getting into sync,[53] this is not for the sake of enjoyment of the music, but in order to become aware of the 'Whole' (the screen) which is within but beyond this music (sense-data in the perceptual field; the film-show).

It is as though you become the singer and also, simultaneously, the player of every instrument (at a concert It is best to sit in the back row because you can get taken up with the music and your movements can upset those sitting behind you). Remember, it is a fact that language is anyway not adequate to the task, the talk is of going 'within but beyond' or 'of transcending' but actually there is nowhere to go, the Whole is here, now, 'nearer than near', the notes are parts, the song is a relationship of parts. The singer may be a soprano or a bass, the backing music may be provided by a baroque ensemble or a rock band it doesn't matter. The pattern or process is the same:

Whole   >   Space Parts Time   >   Whole

The relationship of parts is in space-time, the devotee in following every note with intense concentration is re-creating that relationship i.e., aligning the parts to achieve synchronicity and so becoming aware of the Whole, through union i.e., through experience.

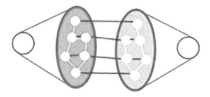

You may be sitting listening to the radio or Hi Fi at home or at the concert and so deliberately positioning yourself into an environment you find conducive for meditating.

The next morning you wake up at 5 am and the first thing you hear are birds singing and then naturally you carry on (as though you were still at the concert) taking this as another opportunity to meditate, even though lying down in bed.

It is good practice and since they are living creatures it is especially sacred and meaningful. It can, however, be hard to get in sync with the bird song. The sound of traffic in the street, however, is much easier to synchronise with; cars, heavy lorries, motor bikes all coming into your perceptual field outside your window stopping at the traffic lights and then starting off, the motor bike especially, changing gear and accelerating, the sound then receding as it gets further off into the distance.

With concentration you make progress, and you get into sync. The sound is within you (it is within you literally, of course, since all sound enters your ear and enters [your] consciousness) and you are, as it were, within the sound.

The motorbike, the road and indeed everything is within the 'Whole'. In your mind, which is in 'space-time', you think of the motor bike as a separate physical object travelling away from you, which, from upbringing and habit, you identify as your body. The sound gradually becomes weaker the further the motorbike proceeds into the distance. However, with meditation you are aware that all of this is superimposed on consciousness.

Although it is true that the 'Whole' is not in space-time, and therefore there is this interface which cannot be understood or described, it is important to remember that the Whole is a given i.e., the Whole Is, Here, Now.

A devotee does not become the 'Whole' but becomes one with the 'Whole'; the 'Whole' already is, forever has been and forever will be.

Within each Part.

Greater than the sum total of Parts.

The same independently of a change in the Parts

The task is to remove the ignorance, which causes the false identification of the Self with the space-time body etc.

The devotee realizes that he/she does not see or hear or do anything, everything is carried out by nature, within space-time. The vibrations of the tympanic membrane, the translation of these vibrations into electrical signals; the

processing that takes place in the brain and so on are all
events in space-time carried out by nature automatically.

The illumined soul Whose heart is Brahman's heart Thinks always: I am doing nothing,' No matter what he sees Hears, touches, smells, eats; No matter whether he is moving, Sleeping, breathing, speaking, Excreting, or grasping something with the hand, or opening his eyes: This he knows always: 'I am not seeing, I am not hearing: It is the senses that see and hear And touch things of the senses.' Prabhavananda and Isherwood (Page 71)	"Nought of myself I do!" Thus, will he think – who holds the truth of truths – In seeing, hearing, smelling; when He eats, or goes, or breathes; slumbers or talks, Holds fast or loosens, opens his eyes or shuts; Always assured "This is the sense-world plays with senses." Sir Edward Arnold (Page 53)

The Self is not the membranes, nerves, brain cells etc. but is
the Whole i.e., consciousness itself; the Self is the screen, not
the film show superimposed on it.

"Do not say: 'God gave us this delusion'. You dream you are the doer, You dream that action is done, You dream that action bears fruit, It is your ignorance, It is the world's delusion That gives you these dreams. The Lord is everywhere And always perfect: What does he care for man's sin Or the righteousness of man? Prabhavananda and Isherwood (page 72/73)	"This world's Lord makes Neither the work, nor passion for the work, Nor lust for fruit of work; the man's own self Pushes to these! The Master of this World Take on himself the good or evil deeds Of no man - dwelling beyond! Mankind errs here By folly, darkening knowledge. Sir Edward Arnold (page 54)

"What does he care for man's sin.
Or the righteousness of man?"

I found these two lines of the verse to be stating the case in no uncertain terms and at first reading, for me, I was rather put off since it implied that God is indifferent entirely; regardless of the rightness or wrongness of the actions human beings take.

I have always felt that it was right to be good rather than bad; kind rather than cruel; thoughtful rather than thoughtless. God however doesn't actually, it seems, give a toss, however, to know God you very certainly do have to be good, not bad, and so on.

The indifference to man's sin or righteousness is not due to a lack of interest or love from God. God is indifferent in the same way as the screen is indifferent to the film show projected onto it; the characters and events in the film show can be good or bad but the screen is always the screen and unaffected. God is God, One, ever all itself, infinite, eternal.

Participants in the film show live out their lives in the film show (the relative reality) which is projected onto the screen (the absolute reality). Life in the relative reality proceeds according to the laws that apply to it i.e., the laws of Nature, Karma, or Society. The participants therefore reap as they sow; make their beds and then lie in them; suffer or enjoy the consequences of their own actions and so on.

Everything good or bad takes place in the film-show and the participants (nearly all of them) are unaware that there is this unseen screen within; the bed rock or the divine ground, the 'screen' which we refer to as God.

To nearly everyone, perhaps, God is not 'Real': because God cannot be seen, grasped hold of and so on and many live in ignorance of God's presence; however, I suspect they would accept that they suffer from a 'lack'; a sense of loneliness; a sense that something is missing.

The vast majority, I believe, think that this is because of a lack of money, possessions or due to the unfavourable circumstances they find themselves in. For many the solution seems to be to undertake activities to acquire money; possessions and so make their circumstances favourable; then they are sure this 'lack' will be dissipated.

I believe however that after achieving all these aims (if indeed it is ever possible i.e., when is enough, enough?) it will still not bring them release from this 'lack'; this sense of loneliness; and this sense that something is missing.

Then still they will ask "Is this all there is"? "Is this as good as it gets"?

This is not helped by realising that they have probably spent the best part of their life to acquire all these riches and perhaps in their desire to do so they have done it on the backs of others and through dishonest practices and so on. It is still progress, in a sense however, because the only proof of anything is the experience of it and having now experienced it, they at least have realised that this route they have been following turns out to have been a dead end.

There may have been people who tried to tell them this right at the beginning and therefore not to waste their time, their life, and so miss out on the real purpose, but these people couldn't give or communicate the experience itself. It may just be that each individual has to find out for themselves i.e. '*No one else will or can do it for you.*

Every human being, I believe feels this sense of isolation; this lack of unity or completeness within and, for me, it is this **lack of unity** that is the creative drive ('the Creator'); the impetus for evolution and responsible for the entire creation.

The relationships of parts' in its entirety (i.e., space-time) changes continuously because of this creative force driving ever onward seeking to return to its former unity.

This applies also to every human being; a participating 'part' within this space-time set of relationships. It is obviously true that every human being has to get out of bed in the morning and work to get what they need but for some this impetus leads them to seek status, power, and wealth in the belief that this inner lack of completeness will then be resolved.

In others, I believe (relatively few), there is no longer this desire or ambition; instead, they seek rather to resolve their lack of completeness through acquiring knowledge and spiritual enlightenment. Some people just want to know what 'the Reality' is; what the Truth is; they may have this objective, for reasons unknown (or perhaps because they are carrying on from where they left off in some previous experience). There are also those perhaps, referred to above, who have been there, done that, got the T shirt and then realised through their own experience that it did not deliver.

Siddhartha Gautama (born 563 BC India) was called 'Buddha ', meaning 'the awakened one' and is the founder of Buddhism. He is said to have lived as a Prince in complete ignorance of the harsh realities of life as lived by normal people outside the walls of the palace'.

A popular biography states, that at the age of 29, Siddhartha left his palace to meet his subjects and despite his father's efforts to hide from him the sick, aged, and suffering, Siddhartha was said to have seen an old man . . .. and so, for the first time was awakened to the fragility of life, of disease, decay, and death and this caused him to leave the palace and his family in search of peace and enlightenment.

As can be seen throughout history, in certain other individuals, at the other end of the character scale from Siddhartha, this inner drive has led to extremes of egotism which have caused various malign political and religious ideologies to develop.

I haven't researched this, but from the top of my head and keeping to events in my life span so far, I can list:

Hitler (and of course numerous fellow Nazis); the Holocaust etc.
Stalin: Communism and the Gulag; the Holodomor in Ukraine.
Hirohito: Treatment of prisoners of war (Burma railway), the Barbarity in China.
Mao Zedong: Communism, the Cultural Revolution, and the famine.
Pol Pot: Communism; the Khmer Rouge and the killing fields.

There are many others (e.g., in Africa) who I have overlooked, or not known about and, of course, currently, or recently, Sadam Hussain in Iraq; Mugabe in Zimbabwe; Kim

Chong-il in North Korea; Gaddafi in Libya. There is also the very active emergence of Islamic terrorism throughout the Middle East and North-eastern Africa such organisations as: Al-Qaeda, Taliban, Hamas, Hezbollah.

At this current time (2023) others can be added to the list e.g., Putin in Russia, Xi Jinping in China, Kim Jong-un in North Korea, Ali Khamenei in Iran etc.... but I think the point has been made so I will leave it there.

Although I am not a church going Christian (I am 'Church of England', but I am a devotee of God as described in this essay). I am often reminded of snippets picked up, perhaps from early days at Sunday school or from general research and reading on spiritual issues e.g., in the context of Islamic fundamentalism etc. the advice 'Ye shall know them by their fruits'[54] springs very much to my mind.

This is not a complete list, not the result of scholarly research, being my subjective view only and off the top of my head. Many argue that the characters and events referred to above e.g., the Holocaust actually show there is no God.

The devotee however needs always to remain focused on God;[55] the screen (which is not IN the film show) and not to be brought down by characters and events in the film show, no matter how difficult this is. The word indifference can be misleading, holy-indifference or dispassion may be more appropriate.

The devotee must have a moral sense about the difference between virtue and vice, its opposite, and therefore try to develop virtue and remove vice in his/her thinking and actions.

For me I take 'moral' to mean being concerned with behaviour that is 'right' rather than 'wrong; 'virtue' being actions or qualities that are good, honourable, decent, respectable, worthy, and so on; 'vice' being actions or qualities that are immoral, wrong, bad, corrupt and the like. I must state I have no expertise with regard to all these matters and they are difficult subjects. I have neglected to mention ethics, but to me to be ethical is probably the same or similar as to be moral, I imagine there may be quite profound philosophical differences but confess to being a layman here.

I cannot be wise about these matters and am not qualified to give advice as to what the devotee should do or not do except to make the very important point that the devotee must take responsibility for his/her own thinking and actions; to perform every action (inwardly; secretly) as worship to God, and not for personal selfish reasons.

I also believe that virtues are not to be pursued because they will make you stand out and kind of glow with goodness but rather, it is because they are necessary for the very practical purpose of making it possible for you to establish union e.g., 'unselfishness' is a prerequisite (as is obvious and just common sense when you think about it).

If you accept that the objective is to remove this false identification of yourself (the screen) to the body, senses etc. (an ego in the film show) then 'unselfishness' is a very necessary virtue which will weaken and help dissolve this false identification and so prepare the way for you reaching union.

At the risk of quoting the Gita' excessively I ought to carry on the sequence of verses quoted above (on page 77).

See next page:

"The Atman is the light:
The light is covered by darkness:
This darkness is delusion:
That is why we dream.

When the light of the Atman
Drives out our darkness
That light shines forth from us,
A sun in splendour,
The revealed Brahman.

The devoted dwell with Him,
They know Him always
There in the heart,
Where action is not.
He is all their aim.
Made free by His Knowledge
From past uncleanness
Of deed or of thought,
They find the place of freedom,
The place of no return.

Seeing all things equal,
The enlightened may look
On the Brahmin,
learned and gentle,
On the cow, on the elephant,
On the dog, on the eater of dogs.

Absorbed in Brahman
He overcomes the world
Even here, alive in the world.
Brahman is one,
Changeless, untouched by evil:
What home have we but him?

Prabhavananda and Isherwood
(page 73/74)

"But, for whom
That darkness of the soul is chased by light,
Splendid and clear shines manifest the
Truth As if a Sun of Wisdom sprang to shed
Its beams of dawn. Him meditating still,
Him seeking, with Him blended,
Stayed on Him,
The souls illuminated take that road
Which hath no turning back
– Their sins flung off by strength of faith.
[Who will may have this Light;
Who hath it sees.] To him who wisely sees,
The Brahman with his scrolls and sanctities,
The cow, the elephant, the unclean dog,
The Outcast gorging dog's meat are all one.
The world is overcome – aye! Even here!
By such as fix their faith on Unity.
The sinless Brahma dwells in Unity,

Sir Edward Arnold (page 54/55)

The task then is to develop even mindedness.

To take up the subject of music again as an example of meditation, I have a natural love of music and feel one of the reasons I was fortunate to have been born in 1944 was that I was 13 or 14 years old when music, for me, really took off: Traditional Jazz, Modern Jazz, Skiffle, Rock and Roll, Blues Rock, Folk Rock, Progressive Rock.

Recently however, over the last few years especially, I have discovered 'Early music', especially music during the period

1600's to late 1700's this is what I refer to as 'Baroque' (I am not a music scholar) but particular favourite composers of mine are Purcell and Bach but there are many others from that period).

I heard somewhere that 'Douglas Adams', the author of *'The Hitchhikers Guide to the Galaxy'* was asked to nominate some music which represents the best we have on earth so that it could be included on a gold platter to be sent into space.

'Voyager 1' after its launch over 36 years ago has been reported in 2013 to have entered Interstellar Space and is (in 2022) about 14.6 billion miles or 23.5 billion kilometres away from earth.

Douglas recommended they must include some 'Bach' but added that it might be seen as 'showing off'. It's an example of his humour but also a fine and fitting testament to Bach's music.

What must be remembered however is that the screen is 'One' and indifferent to mine or your taste in music. It is natural, in all things, to be attracted by the pleasant and repelled by the unpleasant, but in meditation you are aligning your listening to gain experience of the screen.

Music is just vibrating notes or frequencies, although this is true also for Purcell, Handel, Bach and other Baroque or Early composers I wonder whether this Baroque or early music might be particularly conducive to meditation because it has an innate feel and connection to the underlying harmony or natural mathematics of nature; similar perhaps to the influence the 'Golden ratio' (the Divine Proportion) has on what we regard as beautiful in the visual field.[56]

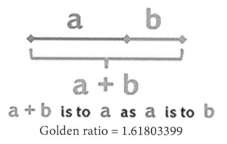

a + b **is to** a **as** a **is to** b
Golden ratio = 1.61803399

Nevertheless, it is important to develop evenness of vision; even mindedness and equality to all i.e., the Self (Capital S), God, Brahman, Atman, Absolute Reality, Consciousness, the Screen is equally present in all vibrating notes or frequencies of sound and vision etc.

One example in my experience came when sitting in a cafe one day, when to my delight the track 'Hey Joe' by Jimmy Hendrix started playing on the music system. This is a track I have always liked (though indifferent to the lyrics) and since I haven't got this on CD at home, I only get to hear it by chance e.g., as was happening in the cafe that day,

I found it very easy to seemingly drop into sync and all was very well (although I was, in hindsight, enjoying the music itself and not so in sync as I should have been to experience the screen within).

Then behind the counter they started to use the steam jet to heat up some milk. This noise was totally dominating and simply filled my perceptual field, blotting out everything else, this bloody noise became my experience and it continued to be until it stopped, at first I tried to retain my composure saying to myself that it might only go on for a few seconds and then the music would be back, however I think they must have been heating up milk in a bucket since the noise went on and on and 'Hey Joe' was well over when eventually it stopped.

It surprised me how much it upset my mood,

Why can't people drink Tea, a tea bag in a mug with boiling water and a little cold milk, quick cheap and quiet, but no, everyone wants to drink latte, cappuccino or whatever, hence the bloody noise, and one of the reasons why so many people are so fat, and why everything takes such a long time.

As a consequence, I was in a bad, irritable mood and it took me a surprisingly long (waste of) time to get control back again, to recollect and return to meditation. Later I realised that the problem was my attachment to that particular track of 'Hey Joe' and that this enjoyment was blotted out so brutally by the noise of the steam.

I would have to develop evenness of mind and equality to all. I should have let the music go, without regret and simply got into sync with the steam-noise-music, it is all just vibrations, the purpose is to be in sync in order to experience the screen, that experience is the goal not the superficial enjoyment of 'Hey Joe' at the sense-data level.

With music the lyrics are not the main issue, the words matter but I'm not listening to them for the sake of the story, indeed a lot of music I listen to, at home or at a concert have lyrics that are not even in English. I have gone to the concert many times to listen to Mozart's Requiem, which is usually sung in German, I believe, it is quite irrelevant to the experience.

Music, general background sound e.g., of traffic and natural sound, the wind in the trees etc. is easy to listen to in a concentrated manner, but people talking is more difficult since it is intrusive to listen in on other peoples conversations.

When this is not an issue, say when sitting on a bus with people talking behind you, there is the problem that the mind will, by default, follow the conversation, which, of course distracts you from the task which is to experience the 'Whole'.

There is a scriptural quote which goes something like *"We are all made in God's image"*, I would prefer to be able to give the formal reference, but don't have it to hand, however for me this is really common sense. It does not mean God looks like a human being.

God is formless. God is the 'Whole', the screen, so nothing whatsoever can exist other than what is projected on it, therefore the image of the screen is reflected back within us all naturally, how can it be otherwise? (The problem of language arises again i.e., how can there be an image of the screen when it is formless, this is not a game of words or intellectual rhetoric, you cannot describe God, that's the way it is, God is not in space-time).

If you listen and achieve synchronicity with the voice that enters your ear you will experience the screen, you will recognize God's image when you do. Whether it's a man's voice or a woman's', a child's or a baby's voice the screen is one, indivisible; it is within every voice as it is within yours, listen out for it.

The same goes for getting into sync visually, look out for it and you will, sooner or later, recognize God's image within others, regardless of their nationality, gender, age, colour, conventional beauty etc.

You need to cease thinking of yourself as this body, obviously this is difficult, you inhabit the body; you are closely associated with it from birth, your gender also, your society, religion or not, and so on as mentioned previously.

You wake up with a headache and this stays with you all day, you have to wash, eat and in all the many other ways tend to your bodily needs, you have to work in some way to earn money, to support yourself and perhaps your family and other relatives, perhaps in a job you hate for a low wage as is the case for many people.

Despite these difficulties come to regard the body (and the senses, the mind, the intellect) as equipment at your disposal, you need to look after it, tend to its needs, work to fulfil your responsibilities and so on, but you need to stand apart from it; take control of it and then live using this equipment to realize your true identity which is one with the 'Whole'.

Music is powerful and easy in meditation because no ego is involved, you can focus on it and give it your concentrated attention without any inhibitions. On many occasions you will benefit from it as a lifeline e.g., you may be in circumstances where you are taken up with events around you and perhaps under stress or in fear, then suddenly you hear music from somewhere and it reminds you to recollect and so become focused again, getting back into sync and bringing your mind back to the awareness that God Is, Here, Now.

It is not only music that links you in this way, the natural sounds which surround you are, in a sense, also music. The next time you are in the cafe and the steam noise blots out music from the radio, recollect and switch your focus (i.e., meditation) seamlessly onto the steam-noise-music, the traffic-in-the-street-music and such like.

The aim first is to make progress; to gain knowledge and enter, or reach, that experience of the screen, and then the aim is to stay there (i.e., Here, Now).

You have to gain control of the mind; the mind it seems is

unceasing in its appetites and will fire off continuously in reaction to sights and sounds and thoughts also to events and ideas in the imagination.

There is a saying that a man thinks of sex every seven seconds or something, this is obviously not true,[57] but it is definitely true that a great deal of your time is spent in your head, so to speak, daydreaming or fantasizing.

Control of the mind is simple i.e., keep focused and in sync then all else will follow but this in practice can be difficult, so you must persist.

Even a mind that knows the path Can be dragged from the path: The senses are so unruly. But he controls the senses. And recollects the mind. And fixes it on me, I call him illumined. Prabhavananda and Isherwood (page 48)	Yet may it chance, O Son of Kunti! that a governed mind Shall some time feel the sense-storms sweep, and wrest. Strong self-control by the roots. Let him regain His Kingdom! Let him conquer this and sit On Me intent. That man alone is wise. Who keeps the mastery of himself! Sir Edward Arnold (page 27)

A devotee gains control of the mind by recollection i.e., continuously, or repeatedly, bringing it back to the task e.g., when I was in the cafe I was angered and frustrated because the steam noise blotted out the music I was enjoying and because I was not in control of my mind it took me off in all sorts of directions:

If people would drink tea like me there wouldn't be this noise, then because the customer wants coffee the barista 'bangs' the metal device on the waste-tin to empty it of used coffee grains before making the next one; with all this noise and banging, sitting in this cafe is like sitting in a factory, the steam stops but then less than a minute later the fridge switches itself on and whirrs irritatingly and noisily away.

I look out the window and see one of those who wear their jeans very low down; I personally don't get this at all, haven't they been able yet to grasp how to wear trousers, despite the obvious discomfort of their trouser crotch being halfway down their thighs, it is obviously deliberate, they remind me of the 'dirty old men' types you used to see around, perhaps they get off on the precariousness of it all? The feeling that at any time ...heavy breathing noises here... their trousers might slip down completely, the up-to-date version perhaps of opening the raincoat to 'flash' in the street.

Perhaps its just that I have a right wing, working class, Tory attitude marking these young men down as YOB's although this may not be the correct technical term since I think it's something to do with Rap, Hip Hop, or a similar music scene. I expect I have got it completely wrong about the wearing of trousers so obviously and inappropriately low. I think it is to give the message that they are hard and cool – man! they are such who are never in the situation where they will need to run away hence wear their trousers so low that running is not a practical possibility, a clear statement to everyone how hard and cool, they are – man! I do think the general quality of life would be improved if they would wear their trousers in the conventional fashion and instead adopt a different method, perhaps wear a lapel badge (dick shaped), this would enable them to recognize each other as hard and cool hip hoppers or whatever when out and about.

*This then leads my mind into thinking about what the term **YOB** stands for, again I don't know but think it stands for '**Y**oung, **O**bnoxious, **B**astard' if so then it's a rich addition to the English language and quite a good description of many.*[58]

Once my mind gets into this vein it can go on for quite some time, after all there is so much to rant on about. I do sometimes realise that I am just in my head and have got things quite wrong.

I recall a particular time when I was feeling happy and free, having just left the army in 1968, when being with some others, long hair, beard, dressed in a 'granddad' vest, blue Royal Navy denim seaman's shirt (the genuine article given me by a seaman from when I spent a few weeks while in the Army on a RN Mine sweeper) and flared cords.

I, along with the others, came across as Hippies and we were looking round Hampton Court – far out! Then what looked like a typical retired Major walked by saying to those he was with "if it was up to me, I would have them horse whipped..."

I felt quite hurt and offended, here I was, a real person I had just spent 10 years in the Army, taken up work in the Simon Community charity, kind, decent, conscientious, and just wonderful in every way and that was his comment?

Am I now when regarding the hard and cool hip hopper, just being the same as the retired army Major type was regarding me, do we just change places?

A long time went by before I settled down and remembered what my purpose was and returned to meditation focusing on the noise the fridge was making.

Doing this I was soon back and realizing the 'Whole' is the same independently of the parts. I resolved to learn from this so that the next time I would not let my mind take me off here, there, and everywhere.

The devotee may/will have to recollect over and over again many times, even sometimes during the space of a single minute, such is the tendency of the mind to wander off.

What a devotee needs, as it were, is to reach the Whole; the screen, even if this is only momentarily. Then the devotee will know that he/she is on the right track and has everything needed to reach that screen, and can eventually, if he/she keeps going, establish union.

This, of course, is the true situation since **only the self can know the Self, no one else will or can do it for you.** If you have become a devotee and practice meditation it is no longer useful or necessary to waste time in your head on argument, speculation, rants about YOB's etc. What you need is to concentrate on getting into sync with what you hear and see because this will bring you the knowledge and experience of the screen.

The man walking along with the peaked hat or hood, trousers halfway down his backside and so on, is responsible for his appearance, his behaviour, his attitude; if he is to be judged then this will be taken care of through the laws of nature and karma, and societal laws too, when applicable.

To the devotee this man is a collection of sense data; his voice sound waves i.e., entering consciousness via synchronised vibrations of the tympanic membrane (ear drum) causing the vibrations of the small ossicle bones in the inner ear and so on as mentioned previously; his appearance or bodily form (including peaked cap etc.) is visual sense data, i.e., light waves or vibrations albeit of a much higher frequency range, entering via the eyes.[59]

This perceived 'set of sense data' has a recognizable name and form: i.e., a 'human being' then in more detail, as applicable, e.g., is a man rather than a woman or a child, is tall, short, fat, thin, African, Indian, Caucasian, Christian, Hindu, Muslim, and so on and on depending on how the collection of sense data is categorised, listed, and sorted.

However, all this detail is irrelevant what matters to the devotee is that this perceived 'set of sense data' is superimposed on the screen i.e., is a manifestation[60] of God.

The devotee knows that God is 'One', omnipresent and equally present in all. By maintaining an even vision towards others, he or she will, sooner or later, recognize God's image within the other. This regardless of whether the other is a man, woman, or a child; is tall, short, fat, or thin, African, Indian, Caucasian, Christian, Hindu, Muslim, and so on.

My face is equal To all creation, Loving no one Nor hating any. Nevertheless, My devotees dwell Within me always: I also show forth And am seen within them. Prabhavananda and Isherwood (page 108)	I am alike for all! I know not hate, I know not favour! What is made is mine! But them that worship Me with love, I love; They are in Me, and I in them! Sir Edward Arnold (page 89)

I am increasingly aware of the importance and the value of meditating on the voice; gaining synchronicity and thereby, bringing awareness of the 'Whole'; of the screen within.

A man's voice or a woman's it doesn't matter, you are not the body; you are not a man nor are you a woman you are the screen.

The more you recollect; the more you become aware; the more you become grounded. When you are listening to a news reader on the TV or radio then with recollection, no matter how disturbing and depressing the news, you remain grounded and do not allow yourself to become unduly disturbed or depressed (not to be confused with a 'couldn't care less' indifference).

"Brahman is the reality - the one existence, absolutely independent of human thought or idea. Because of the ignorance of our human minds, the universe seems to be composed of diverse forms. It is Brahman alone.
A jar made of clay is not other than clay. It is clay essentially. The form of the jar has no independent existence. What, then, is the jar? Merely an invented name! The form of the jar can never be perceived apart from the clay. What, then, is the jar? An appearance! The reality is the clay itself.
This universe is an effect of Brahman. It can never be anything else but Brahman. Apart from Brahman, it does not exist. There is nothing beside Him. He who says that this universe has an independent existence is still suffering from delusion. He is like a man talking in his sleep.
"The universe is Brahman" - so says the great seer of the Atharva Veda. The universe, therefore, is nothing but Brahman. It is superimposed upon Him. It has no separate existence, apart from its ground".

Shankara's Crest Jewel of Discrimination page 67

Having faith of course is necessary and initially, perhaps is the only thing you have to fall back on, but experience through recollection, even just a little, is a very powerful vindication of that faith.

Suddenly, to use an analogy, you part the entangled weed and flotsam floating on the surface of the pond and immediately you see it (it can't be seen literally, of course, but you see that everything reflects that it IS, it is perfect feedback), even though the weed etc. closes together immediately once more to obscure and hide it again.

This experience is private to you but sufficient for you to

avoid being completely brought down by this world, and sufficient to make you want to part the surface layer again.

I put forward previously, that music was communicated over the radio by being superimposed upon a 'carrier frequency' and that to experience that music, here and now, we only needed to tune to the relevant 'carrier frequency', e.g., 94.9 MHz which is BBC London, and by so doing we can hear and experience it.

I now put forward, by way of analogy, that 'God'; the 'Whole'; 'consciousness'; the 'screen' (or whatever term you prefer to use) can be thought of as like the 'supreme carrier frequency' and that space-time frequencies and their evolution are superimposed upon this giving the perceptual field which our sensory organs are receptive to.

However, this 'supreme carrier frequency', of course, does not itself vibrate, has no space-time properties and so cannot be known in the space-time sense of knowing.

We cannot therefore tune in to it, but if we get into sync with the superimposed space-time frequencies e.g., the music, voices, steam-noise-music & visual physical objects etc. We are in effect, tuning in or drilling down and by this means (of meditating) we can experience it. We meditate in the same way when considering sense data entering the eyes.

Tuning in or drilling down when regarding other human beings as sense data phenomenon is difficult, because it is not acceptable to stare with concentration at other people e.g., in the café, on the underground and so on.

The baby, or young child, can get away with such open staring, it is acceptable because it is innocent; because the baby or young child is without ego, but even this can be an uncomfortable experience for some of those stared at.

At the concert or theatre of course, you are a member of the audience, and this provides a good opportunity to watch closely, to follow every movement, to get into sync, to drill down or to surf the sense data waves so to speak.

However, in day-to-day life there is a great deal to meditate on that doesn't involve staring at people, you can meditate on physical objects, in shop windows, on the street, at passing traffic e.g., the sight of the motor bike, the sounds of which you have often meditated on and so you then see what you hear and hear what you see, and this helps to take you again into the screen.

Some favourite and fruitful subjects for me during my meditation were birds e.g., seagulls, rooks etc. watching them on the ground or soaring and gliding in flight.

In my experience I also found it easy and very beneficial to follow the flowing, rippling, fluttering movements of flags in the breeze e.g. on each occasion when going to the station, to wait for the train to arrive on my way to work, I always walked along the platform until I could see the flag flying on top of the adjacent insurance HQ building and immediately the unceasing rippling and flapping of the flag captured my attention and excited the bliss of God within.

Movements of net curtains, peoples clothing and the sway of trees, bushes and hedges etc. are continuously happening and it's easy to get into sync with these, and so become aware and experience the screen.

All this enables you to make progress and become more in touch or grounded in the screen i.e., underlying the 'film show' (the perceptual field).

You do have to make progress also in exploring how to observe other people without being noticeably intrusive or causing them the same uncomfortable experience as the baby or young child causes through staring (magnified somewhat by the fact that you are an adult). This goes against staring at others on the tube as a method of approach.

I project, or imagine, a circular boundary that encompasses the perceptual field. This circular boundary doesn't actually exist, it is just an idea, and it enables me to accept that everything i.e., the perceptual field; all sense-data; everything seen and heard, including other people etc. is superimposed upon this 'screen'; that portion of it, which is available to me within the imaginary circular boundary. The screen is 'One', it has no end or beginning (it is just that I cannot see with the eyes anything beyond the range of the screen available to me).

The screen is the 'Self' (or whatever term you prefer e.g., Whole, Within, God, Brahman, Atman, or Consciousness).

This Self (the screen) is all pervading and eternally unchanging. I focus and identify myself with this Self.

The trick is to realise that the Self or the screen is what you are, you have to lose the sense of being 'I' i.e., lose the identification of the Self with the bodily equipment (this bodily equipment remember, is an integral part of the perceptual field superimposed on the screen). the Self cannot step outside of itself because there is no other; there is not an outside to the Self.

You don't stare at the other trying, as it were to see the Self; the screen within the other, because you are that Self. What you do is hold to the 'One' and get into sync; follow everything, visually and aurally in the perceptual field e.g., you are on the bus and a ladies voice comes across the speaker system telling you what the next stop is and, because you are identified with the screen and you are in sync, this voice is, as it were, your voice i.e., you are united with the Self within the voice.

"All that is has its self in him alone. He is the truth, He is the subtle essence of all. He is the Self. And that, Svetaketu, THAT ART THOU."

"Please , sir, tell me more, about this Self"

"Be it so. Bring a fruit of that Nyagrodha tree."

"Here it is, sir."

"Break it."

"It is broken, sir."

"What do you see?"

"Some seeds, extremely small, sir."

"Break one of them."

"It is broken, sir."

"What do you see?"

"Nothing, sir."

"The subtle essence you do not see, and in that is the whole of the Nyagrodha tree. Believe me, my son, that that which is the subtle essence – in that have all things their existence. That is the truth. That is the Self. And that, Svetaketu, THAT ART THOU."

Extract from the Chandogya: 'The Upanishads' (page 70)

My lord, if this whole earth belonged to me, with all its wealth, should I through its possession attain immortality?

Yagnavalkya
No. Your life would be like that of the rich. None can possibly hope to attain immortality through wealth.

Maitreyi
Then what need have I of wealth? Please, my lord, tell me what you know about the way to immortality.

Yagnavalkya
Dear to me have you always been, Maitreyi, and now you ask to learn of that truth which is nearest my heart. Come, sit by me. I will explain it to you. Meditate on what I say.
　　　It is not for the sake of the husband, my beloved, that the husband is dear, but for the sake of the Self.
　　　It is not for the sake of the wife, my beloved, that the wife is dear, but for the sake of the Self.
　　　It is not for the sake of the children, my beloved, that the children are dear but for the sake of the Self.
　　　It is not for the sake of the wealth, my beloved, that wealth is dear, but for the sake of the Self.
....
It continues.
....
　　　It is not for the sake of itself, my beloved, that anything whatever is esteemed, but for the sake of the Self.

The Self, Maitreyi, is to be known. Hear about it, reflect upon it, meditate upon it. By knowing the Self, my beloved, through hearing, reflection, and meditation, one comes to know all things......

Extract from the Brihadaranyaka: 'The Upanishads (page 86)

I include this other extract as well, from the 'Chandogya' Upanishad, not only because it is relevant but also because when I first read it, I was impressed that this was written such a long time ago several hundred years before Christ and probably before the Bhagavad Gita (500 years BC) came into being.

What impressed me is that, at the time this was written I don't imagine there was any knowledge concerning the structure of matter. If you take anything you can break it down into its component parts, and in turn break each component part to reveal yet another relationship of parts:

e.g., the cell >> molecule >> atom >> particle >> quarks to eventually arrive at the subtle essence i.e., the 'That art Thou' referred to above, the Whole, the clear light of the void, the Self, Brahman. ...

As discussed earlier everything in creation, from the Big Bang on, and of course, including the Nyagrodha tree, is an evolved relationship of parts; a manifestation of this subtle essence (the Self).

My apologies for the repetition but to reiterate: the approach I take to meditating eyes open, is that wherever I am, I imagine a circular boundary surrounding and defining the limits of my perceptual field e.g., as previously described when I mentioned leaving the kitchen and moving into the garden.

In saying I imagine a circular boundary I mean I just recollect and become conscious that I am in the centre of my perceptual field. There is no boundary; see also the diagrams that show the evolution of the 'particle' to the 'atom'. Here the 'atom' is defined as a relationship of 'particles' contained within a circle; the circle doesn't exist, but it is necessary for visualisation purposes.

Perception is limited, in the sense, that it operates only within certain frequency ranges and amplitudes e.g., the motorcycle accelerates away and proceeds into the distance and eventually it travels beyond the sense of hearing i.e., the amplitude of these vibrations become so reduced that the senses can no longer pick them up; it doesn't cross a circular boundary; there is no edge.

On leaving the house, for example I consciously look up and outward to take in everything as far as I can see, I notice birds flying in the sky, an aircraft so high and far away that I can only see its vapour trails, and consciously I take note that everything seen and heard comprises the perceptual field and this field is superimposed on the whole i.e., the Many in the One.

The One is the screen; I identify myself with this i.e., with consciousness; pure consciousness, consciousness itself. I don't know what the scientific description or explanation of consciousness is but suspect it may be thought of as a product of brain activity, but consciousness is not created, has not evolved, and cannot be modified,[61] nor destroyed (consciousness is the Whole, the Within, the Self, God, Brahman, Atman, the Screen) it is omnipresent and distinct.

I just naturally accept this; perhaps it is an example of 'a priori'[62] knowledge.

Ask yourself wherever you are, on looking around, where does consciousness start? Where does it end? Where is the centre?

You realize that there is no start, end, or centre, you cannot even point to consciousness, your hand and the pointing finger is itself superimposed on it i.e., you cannot touch it, or reach it, consciousness is the screen.

There are two approaches to take.
1) The **Many** within the **One**.   2) The **One** within the **Many**.

Switching between the two until there is no distinction i.e., the two become identical, the mind becomes still, the One alone is.

When through the practice of yoga, the mind ceases its restless movements, and becomes still, he realizes the Atman. It satisfies him entirely. Then he knows that infinite happiness which can be realized by the purified heart but is beyond the grasp of the senses. He stands firm in this realization. Because of it, he can never again wander from the inmost truth of his being.

Now that he holds it
He knows this treasure.
Above all others: Faith so certain
Shall never be shaken.
By heaviest sorrow.

Prabhavananda and Isherwood (page 82)

When mind broods placid, soothed with holy wont: When self contemplates Self, and in itself Hath comfort;
when it knows the nameless joy
Beyond all scope of sense, revealed to soul.
Only to soul! and, knowing, wavers not,
True to the farther Truth; when, holding this,
It deems no other treasure comparable,
But, harboured there,
cannot be stirred or shook.
By any gravest grief, call that state "peace,"

Sir Edward Arnold (page 63)

For I am Brahman
Within this body,
Life immortal
That shall not perish:
I am the Truth
And the Joy for ever.

Prabhavananda and Isherwood (page 110)

Strategies

I found It necessary to have a range of strategies, which I used as inspiration to get me back on the path, I found that what works one day doesn't sometimes work the next.

Regaining control of the mind i.e., to get it back on track gets easier as you go along. In earlier stages it is hard work, thinking through the arguments, step by step, finding new strategies, overcoming the periods of despondency, and overcoming the feeling it is not possible to keep the effort up.

It is important to stress that sometimes these barren periods may be part of the process, from my own experience I think that this can be due to the interrelationship of the gunas (*"sometimes one guna is predominant; sometimes another; and a man's mood and character vary accordingly"* (see Note 35).

There is the obvious possibility that the interactions of the gunas can produce an effect inside by relating together in a manner to depress the spirits, similar to the effect caused outside, by black clouds moving across the sky to obscure the sun.

However, even though this might make us depressed we do know that the sun has not gone away or has ceased to be; we know that we have to carry on and it's certain that sometime soon the sun will come into view again, so its important to keep on going.

An additional possibility is that our periods of fallowness are due to some inner re-organization (of the internal relationships etc.) and while this is happening it's as though we've been disconnected.

The important thing for the devotee is to keep going, remembering that the One Is, Here, Now (no right effort you make is ever wasted). Your efforts and your continued meditation and your continued faith will be rewarded with enlightenment (this is the point I am making).

The inner readjustments, if that was the cause, when completed, result in you becoming re-connected, as it were. Then suddenly you are back on track and your experience is often stronger and deeper than before. Everything slots into place, and you have an ecstatic experience, and you realise again that this is it, or rather that it IS. I am pretty certain there is a leap forward; perhaps it's like all the benefits of your effort during the fallow period, were just held up and then, suddenly they arrive all at once.

I also think this may be just my imagined theory, it may of course just be the joy of making contact again, like when you have been unwell, perhaps a headache which has been with you night and day for two days wears off and stops and then you experience bliss (i.e., which is just because you do not have the headache anymore).

There is also the situation where it is not the interplay of gunas or an inner re-organisation that is the cause but is simply that you are neglecting to recollect.

It is probable that you may lapse many times, go off into your head or like a reformed ex-alcoholic go off on a serious bout of drinking. After sobering up there is the strong feeling that you have blown it utterly and lost it and you give up on it.

Then despite everything, sooner or later (it could even be years later). Something happens which returns you to the task; possibly you take out the 'Bhagavad Gita' from the bookshelf and read a verse and it wakes you up, so to speak or one day you are sitting in the café and music starts playing e.g., in my case it could be 'Hey Jo' by 'Jimmy Hendrix' and it is this that may suddenly take me back and awaken me again to the Self.

There is an experience of bliss which is accompanied by a strong feeling of gratitude and the feeling that you have come home after a long time away.

You realise that you have been completely forgiven; you realise that you haven't blown it with God in the slightest; it is just that you went off. God never goes off: God Is, (Infinitely) Here, (Eternally) Now.

I think it's very important again to stress that (assuming you go through similar experiences as I have) that you can be flying very high one moment and then very low an instant later, conversely of course, and this is the powerful advice to remember, you can be depressed and very low and the strategies or thoughts which previously got you back on track don't work in the slightest and indeed appear pretty stupid in retrospect and you then have doubts about everything.

However then, in an instant everything comes flooding back, it may be because you think back over events and the memory restores you back to the task (last thing at night I have a habit of retracing my day and this is a good habit to try out yourself). It may be because you see or hear something e.g., music playing, or it may be due to grace i.e., apparently undeserved.

It may be because you just give up. The process of looking and trying can itself chase the experience away i.e., you cannot see for looking. You have left the 'Here and Now' behind and so, of course, you are not going to reach it, like a dog trying to catch its own tail it can never do so. When you give up, you stop looking and then realize you are back 'Here and Now'. These are poor explanations; however, you have to do it for yourself; all I am trying to do is to stimulate you to do so.

Example strategies employed:

1. Two revolving perforated disks, both identical in actual fact but revolving out of phase with each other. One light source shining through the perforations in the first disk creates ever-changing patterns of light and shade,

    Then the same light (being present or absent due to its passage through the first disk) passes through the revolving second disk.

    This results in a new generation of ever-changing patterns of light and shade, which are uniquely individual and cut off or separated from the source.

    Imagine what is revealed when the revolutions of the second disk are brought into sync (through meditation) with those of the first, then there is no separation, and it is realised that there is but One light.

    Sense data entering the brain via the sensory organs (e.g., eyes and ears) via the nervous system are related together in the mind to give us our model or representation of the perceptual field (the regularly perceived causes).

Remember however that the perceptual field is a projection of our mind (it is the effect of causes which determine our interpretation of the causes).

One scenario I have used is to regard the external world (the perceptual field) to be the mind of God (i.e., the first disk) and then I align my mind (the second disk) accordingly. I follow every note of the music, i.e. I get into sync, as previously discussed. This aligns the revolving second disk (my mind) with the revolving first disk (God's mind) and so brings experience of the one light i.e., union.

2. When you throw a stone up and forward, as high as you can, it will take a parabolic or curved path, the stone will consume its upward velocity until it falls to zero and is at rest i.e., the stones upward force being matched exactly by the downward force of gravity.

   Gravity, of course, continues to operate therefore the stone starts on its journey back down and returns, following its curved path, gaining its former velocity until it arrives back at ground level. With practice at throwing: a greater distance, height and duration is achieved but always there is the return.

   However, it is possible for the stone to reach so high that it reaches a place where there is no return, the stone still responds to gravity and follows the curved path of return but because of its height its curved path is parallel to the curvature of the earth and so it never returns to ground level, if it can still be considered as falling, then it is falling into itself. The stone if it is synchronised with the earth's rotation, will always remain in the same relative position i.e., in 'geostationary orbit'. This is an analogy which I have used to aid my meditation; I project myself (consciously looking up and outward as above mentioned) forwards and upwards like the stone to take me beyond the pull of sense objects and so escape the gravitational force, so to speak, which normally keeps me confined and tied to the perceptual field. You can then, as it were, see the Many in the One (there is nothing supernatural about this I mean you are not in orbit looking down at this world, by escaping the gravitational force I mean you can be experiencing unity and perhaps bliss when you are just walking down the street stepping over the litter and so on, however you are aware of the One and struck by the beauty of the perceptual field which is superimposed upon that One).

3. A diamond (representing the totality of space-time) has many facets on its surface, each facet cut at a different angle. The surface of some facets may be sparklingly clean and transparent; in others the surface may be opaque with layers of ingrained dirt. Some facets may contain internal spots where the structure is flawed and damaged but in some others the structure is highly integrated and symmetrical.
The One (source) light shining through the diamond will be reflected by the various cuts and angles of the facets resulting in a multitude of colours. Here and there the light is reflected only dimly and, in some facets, possibly not reflected at all.
Occasionally and rarely, there is a facet where the cut, the angle, the internal symmetry, and the surface cleanliness come together to maximum effect, letting the light shine through without any attenuation or refraction i.e., pure, 100% itself. (So, in people and all other phenomenon good or bad there is one light shining through and that is the Self).

There is much more to say which may be helpful. Even eating correctly is difficult e.g. How much to eat? If you do not eat enough, you don't have the health and energy and hence the clarity of thought. If you eat too much your awareness and spirits sink. I have not researched this but assume that after eating; the flow of blood is diverted to the organs of digestion and so less flows to the brain.

From experience I would recommend you eat little but enough (so very difficult to get right). In cafes, therefore you have to ask for small portions, even though you will still probably pay the same standard price. I am not vegetarian I did try this once, but it requires a lot of attention and effort since you cannot live on cheese sandwiches and chips alone. I used to think it was not very spiritual to eat animals but as a devotee you eat to live; everything in moderation; everything an offering to God.

I recommend you read the Bhagavad-Gita and Shankara for everything you need to know, e.g., re the issue of eating it has the following advice:

> *"Men of sattwa like foods which increase their vital force, energy, strength, and health. Such foods add to the pleasure of physical and mental life. They are juicy, soothing, fresh, and agreeable. But men of rajas prefer foods, which are violently bitter, sour, salty, hot, pungent, acid and burning. These cause ill health, and distemper of the mind and body. And men of tamas take a perverse pleasure in foods, which are stale, tasteless, rotten, and impure. They like to eat the leavings of others."*

"Yoga is not for the man who overeats, or for him who fasts excessively. It is not for him who sleeps too much, or for the keeper of exaggerated vigils. Let a man be moderate in sleep and in wakefulness. He will find that yoga takes away all his unhappiness".	"Religion is not his who too much fasts Or too much feasts, nor his who sleeps away An idle mind; nor his who wears to waste His strength in vigils. Nay, Arjuna! Call That true piety which most removes Earth-aches and ills, where one is moderate In eating and in resting, and in sport; measured in wish and act; sleeping betimes, Waking betimes for duty......."
Prabhavananda and Isherwood (page 82)	Sir Edward Arnold (page 62)

These verses above show on the one hand, how the path is only common sense and within the capabilities of everyone; nothing special is required; except that 'you must be true to yourself' and practice 'moderation in all things.

If you do meditate and get into sync and so gain experience of the screen you will find out everything yourself. Feedback will guide you. Reading the Bhagavad-Gita, the Crest Jewel of Discrimination and hopefully reading this essay will encourage, inspire, and help you. It is true however, as stated before that 'No one else will, or can do it for you'.

See next page for extract from 'Shankara's Crest – Jewel of Discrimination' on the theme:

"Such is Brahman, and "That art Thou". Meditate upon this truth".

Caste, creed, family, and lineage do not exist in Brahman. Brahman has neither name nor form; it transcends merit and demerit;
it is beyond time, space, and the objects of experience.
Such is Brahman, and "That art Thou". Meditate upon this truth.

It is untouched by those six waves - hunger, thirst, grief, delusion, decay, and death - which sweep the ocean of worldliness. He who seeks union with it must meditate upon it within the shrine of the heart. It is beyond the grasp of the senses. The intellect cannot understand it. It is out of the reach of thought.
Such is Brahman, and "That art Thou", Meditate upon this truth.

It is the ground upon which this manifold universe, the creation of ignorance, appears to rest. It is its own support. It is neither the gross nor the subtle universe. It is indivisible. It is beyond comparison.
Such is Brahman, and "That art Thou", Meditate upon this truth.

It is free from birth, growth, change, decline, sickness, and death. It is eternal. It is the cause of the evolution of the universe, its preservation, and its dissolution.
Such is Brahman, and "That art Thou", Meditate upon this truth.

It knows no differentiation or death. It is calm, like a vast, waveless expanse of water. It is eternally free and indivisible.
Such is Brahman, and "That art Thou", Meditate upon this truth.

Though one, it is the cause of the many. It is the one and only cause, no other beside it. It has no cause but itself. It is independent, also, of the law of causation. It stands alone.
Such is Brahman, and "That art Thou", Meditate upon this truth.

It is unchangeable, infinite, and imperishable. It is beyond Maya and her effects. It is eternal, undying bliss. It is pure.
Such is Brahman, and "That art Thou", Meditate upon this truth.

It is that one Reality which appears to our ignorance as a manifold universe of names and forms and changes. Like the gold of which many ornaments are made, it remains in itself unchanged.
Such is Brahman, and "That art Thou", Meditate upon this truth.

There is nothing beyond it. It is greater than the greatest. It is the innermost self, the ceaseless joy within us. It is absolute existence, knowledge, and bliss. It is endless, eternal.
Such is Brahman, and "That art Thou", Meditate upon this truth.

Meditate upon this this truth, following the arguments of the scriptures by the aid of reason and intellect. Thus, you will be freed from doubt and confusion, and realise the truth of Brahman. This truth will become as plain to you as water held in the palm of your hand."

Prabhavananda Swami & Isherwood Christopher Shankara's Crest-Jewel of Discrimination. Page 71

I end here but include a bit more from the Bhagavad-Gita to leave you with.

Know this, O Prince: Of things
created all are come forth.
From the seeming union
Of Field and Knower,
Prakriti with Brahman.

Who sees his Lord Within every
creature, deathlessly dwelling
Amidst the mortal:

Thus, ever aware
Of the Omnipresent
Always about him,
He offers no outrage to his own
Atman. Hides the face of God.
Beneath ego no longer:
Therefore, he reaches
That bliss which is highest.

Who sees all action Ever performed
alone by Prakriti.
That man sees truly:
The Atman is actless.

Who sees the separate
Lives of all creatures
United in Brahman
Brought forth from Brahman.
Himself finds Brahman.

Not subject to change
Is the infinite Atman,
Without beginning, beyond the
gunas: Therefore, O Prince
Though it dwells in the body,
It acts not, nor feels
The fruits of our action.

For, like the ether. Pervading all
things. Too subtle for taint,
This Atman also inhabits all bodies
but never is tainted.

By the single sun this world is
illuminated: By its one Knower
The Field is illuminated.

Who thus perceives
With the eye of wisdom
In what manner the Field
Is distinct from its Knower,
How men are made free
From the toils of Prakriti:
His aim is accomplished,
He enters the Highest.

Prabhavananda and Isherwood
(Page 137/139)

Wherever, Indian Prince! Life is – of moving
things, or things unmoved,
Plant or still seed – know, what is there hath
grown by bond of Matter and of Spirit:
Know He sees indeed who sees in all alike
The living, lordly Soul; the Soul supreme,
Imperishable amid the Perishing:
For, whoso thus beholds, in every place,
In every form, the same, one, Living Life,
Doth no more wrongfulness unto himself,
But goes the highest road, which brings to
bliss. Seeing, he sees, indeed, who sees the
mass Of separate living things – each of its
kind – Issue from One,
and blend again to One:
Then hath he Brahma, he attains!

O Prince!
That Ultimate, High Spirit, Uncreate,
Unqualified, even when it entereth flesh
Taketh no stain of acts, worketh in nought!
Like to th' ethereal air, pervading all,
Which, for sheer subtlety, avoideth taint,
The subtle Soul sits everywhere, unstained:
Like to the light of the all-piercing sun
[Which is not changed by aught it shines upo
The Soul's light shineth pure in every place;
And they who, by such eye of wisdom, see
How matter, and what deals with it, divide:
And how the Spirit and the flesh have strife,
Those wise ones go the way which leads to
Life!

Sir Edward Arnold (Page 141/142)

Bibliography

Soanes Catherine & Hawker Sara, **Compact Oxford English Dictionary of Current English**
(Oxford University Press, Third edition. 2005)

Honderich Ted, The **Oxford Companion to Philosophy**
(Oxford University Press, Second edition, 2005)

Teilhard De Chardin Pierre, The **Phenomenon of Man**
(Collins, 1961) *

In his posthumously published book, The Phenomenon of Man, Teilhard writes of the unfolding of the material cosmos, from primordial particles to the development of life, human beings and the noosphere, and finally to his vision of the Omega Point in the future, which is "pulling" all creation towards it. He was a leading proponent of orthogenesis, the idea that evolution occurs in a directional, goal driven way, argued in terms that today go under the banner of convergent evolution. Teilhard argued in Darwinian terms with respect to biology, and supported the synthetic model of evolution, but argued in Lamarckian terms for the development of culture, primarily through the vehicle of education
http://en.wikipedia.org/wiki/Pierre_Teilhard_de_Chardin

Huxley Julian. **The Humanist Frame**
(London Allen & Unwin. 1961)*

Koehler Wolfgang. **Gestalt Psychology**
(G. Bell & Sons: London, 1930) *

Hirst Reginald. **The Problems of Perception**
(George Allen & Unwin,1959) *

Brain Walter. **Mind, Perception and Science**
(Blackwell Scientific Publishing, Oxford, 1961) *

Morris Charles. **Locke, Berkeley, and Hume**
(Oxford University Press, 931) *

Barbour Ian. **Issues in Science and Religion**
(S.C.M. Press, 1966) *

Medawar Peter. **Critical Notice**
(Mind – Oxford University Press – LXX: 99 – 106, 1961) *

Tillich Paul. **Systemic Theology Vol 3: Life and the Spirit**
(The University of Chicago Press, 1976) *

Rees Martin. **Just Six Numbers -The Deep Forces that Shape the Universe**
(Weidenfield & Nicholson, 2000)

Greene Brian. **The Elegant Universe – Superstrings, Hidden Dimensions & the Quest for the Ultimate Theory**
(Jonathan Cape, London, 1999)

Gribbin John. **In Search of Schrödinger's Cat – Quantum Physics and Reality**
(Black Swan, 1991)

Primack Joel & Abrams Nancy. **The View from the Centre of the Universe**
(Fourth Estate, London, 2006)

Huxley Aldous. **The Perennial Philosophy**
(Chatto & Windus, London, 1980)

Arnold Sir Edward. **The Bhagavad-Gita The Song Celestial**
(Watkins Publishing, 2005)

Prabhavananda Swami & Isherwood Christopher.
Bhagavad-Gita, – The Song of God
(Vedanta Press, 3rd Ed 1980)

Prabhavananda Swami & Isherwood Christopher.
Shankara's Crest-Jewel of Discrimination
(A Mentor book from New American Library. 1970)

Prabhavananda Swami & Manchester Frederick. **The Upanishads**
(Signet Classic New American Library 2002)

- NB: Books marked * are included because they are 'references' to an essay written by me in 1970 to gain entry to University as a mature candidate. The essay had the title: 'The Evolution of Consciousness' which I realised after it was handed in, to be a daft title since (as this essay is at pains to explain) consciousness itself does not evolve. It is the human being that evolves and as a result becomes more conscious, and indeed, if choosing to become a devotee, will continue to evolve and so become more conscious and eventually become conscious of consciousness itself i.e., union. The original essay of 1970 is simplified and forms the basis of Chapter (Whole and the Parts) and chapter (The Creation as a Book). These books may be difficult to get hold of, and I mark them * since I don't think reading them is necessary or particularly relevant. Whereas other books listed are very necessary and very beneficial to read, especially these three: The Bhagavad Gita; Crest – Jewel of Discrimination and the Perennial Philosophy

Other books along the way and highly recommended.

Kahlil Gibran. **The Prophet**
(Heinemann: London reprinted 1967)

Hermann Hesse. **Siddhartha**
 (Picador published by Pan Books 1973)

Prabhavananda Swami **Srimad Bhagavatam. – The Wisdom of God**
(Ramakrishna Vedanta Centre, Bourne End, Bucks, SL8 5LG)

Robert M. Pirsig. **Zen and the Art of Motorcycle Maintenance: An Inquiry into Values**
(Harper Torch; Reprint edition (April 25, 2006)

Appendix

A Man For All Seasons – a film by Fred Zinneman (winner of 6 Academy awards) from the play by Robert Bolt. (1966)

Thomas More	Paul Scofield
Alice	Wendy Hiller
Margaret	Susannah York
Roper	Coren Redgrave
Duke of Norfolk	Nigel Davenport
Henry VIII	Robert Shaw
Cromwell	Leo McKern
Richard Rich	John Hurt
Cardinal Wolsey	Orson Welles

This film made a very great impression on me and for me is the best film I have ever seen, on every level e.g., exemplary cast; story based on historical truth, quality of photography, profundity of dialogue, beauty, and stature of the actors.

If I had ever been in a position to meet Paul Scofield, I would have apologised to him because I never wanted to see him as anything else, so never, afterwards, went to a film or theatre play in which he was acting, and didn't therefore contribute to his upkeep and financial success. However, I felt he was holding his own. I didn't want to see his portrayal as Thomas More as just another act, for me it was of life changing significance and it was also a matter of love, I mean non-sexual love.

There is an important distinction between Thomas More as portrayed in this film and the historical Thomas More, I did read up on him and about his work Utopia, but he was, I believe, religious in the strict fundamentalist sense.

My respect and love arose for the man as portrayed in this film, perhaps it is Robert Bolt who has my love, since he was responsible for the play and the dialogue whereas Paul Schofield put it into practice.

What really got to me was that there had indeed been such

a man as Thomas More alive on this earth who was true to his Self, to the extent that he held out against all the pressures on him leading eventually to his social and financial ruin and ultimately to having his head cut of. Whenever I go that way to Tower Hill tube station I stop at the site where he was beheaded. If I ever visit the Tower of London, it will be with his former stay there very much in mind, I will watch the film yet again and research beforehand, to determine where he spent his time e.g., the Bell tower? And when shuffling through it I would be looking intently for some mark or sign, the equivalent of 'I was here' scratched on the wall. The lesson perhaps for me was that this man knew that there was an 'inner Self' and that it is more important than anything else, social status, wealth and even life itself, to be true to that Self, and if he could, then so could I.

Thomas More to Duke of Norfolk
"Affection goes as deep in me as in you, I think but only God is love right through Howard and that's my self". "I will not give in because I oppose it, not my pride, not my spleen, nor any other of my appetites but I do..."
    "Is there in the midst of all this muscle, no sinew that serves no appetite but Norfolk's but is just Norfolk that is..."

Duke of Norfolk
"I'm not a scholar, I don't know whether the marriage was lawful or not but dammit Thomas, look at these names why can't you do as I did and sign – for fellowship..."

Thomas More
"And when we die, and you are sent to heaven for doing your conscience and I am sent to Hell for not doing mine. Will you come with me? For fellowship."

In the Tower: Margaret
"God more regards the thoughts of the heart than the words of the mouth or so you've always told me.

Thomas More "Yes"

Margaret
"Then say the words of the oath and in your heart think otherwise".

Thomas More
"What is an oath then but words we say to God". "When a man takes an oath, he's holding his own self in his own hands like water and if he opens his fingers then, he needn't hope to find himself again."

Margaret
"... In any state that was half good you would be raised up high not here for what you've done already, it's not your fault the state's three quarters bad".

Thomas More "No"

Margaret
"But if you let to suffer for it, you let yourself a hero"

Thomas More
"But look now, if we lived in a state where virtue was profitable, common sense would make us saintly, but since we see that avarice, anger, pride, stupidity commonly profit far beyond charity, modesty, justice and thought, perhaps we must stand fast a little even at the risk of being heroes."

Margaret
"But in reason haven't you done as much as God could reasonably want?"

Thomas More
"Well finally Meg, it isn't a matter of reason finally it is a matter of love.

Notes

1 God is defined as the creator and supreme ruler of the universe (OUP dictionary), the term Brahman or Atman (meaning the ultimate reality underlying all phenomena) is better, however I use the term God from habit, but also, I use other terms e.g., Consciousness, the screen etc.

2 Brahman is the total Godhead, it can never be defined or expressed. The Upanishads say that Brahman is Existence, Knowledge, and Bliss; but these are not attributes. Brahman cannot be said to exist. Brahman is existence itself. Brahman is not wise or happy, but absolute knowledge, absolute Joy.
(Aldous Huxley). Bhagavad-Gita, page 175

3 Atman is a term of convenience. Brahman being absolutely present is within all creatures and objects. The Godhead is present in man, in the mouse, in the stone, in the flash of lightening. Thus considered, Brahman is called the Atman.
(Aldous Huxley). Bhagavad-Gita, page 175

4 The Bhagavad-Gita is available in many translations. The ones I have used and recommend are:
a Prabhavananda Swami & Isherwood Christopher (introduction by Aldous Huxley). Bhagavad-Gita, The Song of God
(Vedanta Press., 3rd edition. 1980)
b Arnold Sir Edward (introduction by Alan Jacobs) The Bhagavad-Gita The Song Celestial
(Watkins Publishing, 2005)
From the introduction by Alan Jacobs:
"This splendid scripture was placed in the centre of the Mahabharata, the epic history of ancient India, so as to be made available to the populace at large as well as

Brahmanic scholars. It is believed to have been composed in the fifth century BC.
Prince Arjuna is greatly troubled when he becomes involved in a civil war and realises, he may have to kill his own teachers and kinsman. But the Divine Messenger Lord Krishna is at hand as Arjuna's chariot driver, and throughout the eighteen incisive chapters he delivers a series of spiritual discourses to dispel all Arjuna's anxieties. He also imparts the quintessential Self Knowledge that will lead to his Self Realisation".

c   Prabhavananda Swami & Isherwood Christopher. Shankara's Crest-Jewel of Discrimination (Viveka Chudamani)
    (A Mentor book from New American Library. 1970)
    From Wikipedia
    The Viveka Chudamani, literally "The Crest-Jewel of Wisdom" is a famous work by Adi Shankara that expounds advaita vedanta philosophy. It has the form of dialogue between the master and the disciple, where the master explains to the disciple the nature of the Atman and the ways to research and know the Atman. The book takes the disciple through step-by-step instructions to reach Brahman.
    NB: See also.
    Eknath Easwaran. The Bhagavad Gita.
                                    (Nilgiri Press. 2011)
    I have recently read this translation and recommend it because of its readability and the introduction to the Gita and to each chapter in turn.

5   I use this word 'ego' to mean 'self-image' i.e., yourself, in the neutral sense, identified as your body, senses, mind, and intellect not to mean 'ego' in the sense of being selfish, narcissistic, vain, or self-important.

6   *"'Love the Lord your God with all your heart and with all your soul and with all your strength and with all your mind'; and 'Love your neighbour as yourself.'" The Bible Luke 10:27*

7   "The set of all events occurring in space and time, like the explosion of a firecracker or the snapping of one's fingers. Space-time is four – dimensional, in that each event can be located by four numbers, three for its position and one for its time of occurrence."
(The Oxford Companion to Philosophy 2nd edition OUP)

8   *"When the vision of Reality comes, the veil of ignorance is completely removed. As long as we perceive things falsely, our false perception distracts us and makes us miserable. When our false perception is corrected, misery ends also.*
For example, you see a rope and think it is a snake. As soon as you realise that the rope is a rope, your false perception of a snake ceases, and you are no longer distracted by the fear it inspired. Therefore, the wise man who wishes to break his bondage must know the Reality."
Shankara (Crest – Jewel of Discrimination) page 84

9   I am not able to define love but it's nothing to do with the physical/sexual meaning (in God the lover, the love and the beloved become One).
Without love there is no union with God, I understood that one has to love God but never knew how one could do this, it's not like I could take out my love and switch it on. I used to think how can I love; Do I have any? Where is it? and so on.
Aldous Huxley has assembled a whole chapter regarding this issue (chapter 3 – Charity, The Perennial Philosophy). The following extract is an example (taken from Jean Pierre Camus)
"I once asked the Bishop of Geneva what one must do to attain Perfection. 'You must love God with all your heart, 'he answered, 'and your neighbour as yourself.'
'I did not ask wherein perfection lies,' I rejoined,' but how to attain it.' 'Charity,' he said again, 'that is both the means and the end, the only way by which we can reach that perfection which is, after all, but Charity itself…. Just as the soul is the life of the body, so charity is the life of the soul.'

'I know all that,' I said. 'But I want to know how one is to love God with all one's heart and one's neighbour as oneself.'

But again, he answered, 'We must love God with all our hearts, and our neighbour as ourselves.'

'I am no further than I was,' I replied. 'Tell me how to acquire such love.

'The best way, the shortest and easiest way of loving God with all one's heart is to love Him wholly and heartily!'

He would give no other answer. At last, however, the Bishop said, 'There are many besides you who want me to tell them of methods and systems and secret ways of becoming perfect, and I can only tell them that the sole secret is a hearty love of God, and the only way of attaining that love is by loving. You learn to speak by speaking, to study by studying, to run by running, to work by working; and just so you learn to love God and man by loving. All those who think to learn in any other way deceive themselves. If you want to love God, go on loving him more and more. Begin as a mere apprentice, and the very power of love will lead you on to become a master in the art. Those who have made most progress will continually press on, never believing themselves to have reached their end; for charity should go on increasing until we draw our last breath."

Jean Pierre Camus

As already mentioned, God is the screen, you, and everyone else (including all space-time) is superimposed on this screen and through right action and right meditation you become more aware of the screen's presence and this awareness causes you to experience love and to go on increasing this love as your experience deepens.

10   Present everywhere, at the same time (OUP dictionary).

11   I recall the time when I was staying in a friends place, bedding down on the floor in the front room. During the night in the gloom (the room getting some light from the

street lighting coming through the window). I rolled a cigarette and then struck a match.

This gave me an 'insight', a realisation and (in my sense of the word) a spiritual experience.

The match burst into flame and after lighting the roll up I watched it burn. It was an event in the perceptual field, the whole room was lit up in a flickering manner of light and shadow.

I realised for the first time (I had of course struck matches to light roll ups many, many times in my life up until then) that the match was burning in my field of vision i.e., in consciousness yet the consciousness itself was not affected in any way.

Of course, if I was to hold my hand over the flame there would be an experience of pain and there would be burn damage to the tissues, but (although this is the very hard thing to accept) the hand, the body, the senses, the mind, and the intellect is in the same way a relationship of parts within this perceptual field. The parts interact with other parts in the relationship i.e., the flame will burn the tissues of my hand, nerve sensors embedded in these tissues will send signals to my brain and as a result of processing in my brain, messages will be sent resulting in the reflex action of removing my hand away from the flame, at the same time causing me to shout, or swear out loud.

Consciousness itself however is unaffected, Consciousness is the 'Whole' which is greater than the sum total of parts.

12 I experienced the Self i.e., distinct from everything phenomenal (the body, that which is seen, heard, felt and so on). I mean utterly distinct.

That I was associated however with this specific intellect, mind, senses, and body in a more intimate and different manner than with anything else seen and heard (I was of course born into this relationship of parts; into this phenomenal world just until, I could meditate and then arrive at this awareness of having nothing to do with it).

Once again, I realised that I had been thinking this and

saying this and knowing this for a long time, intellectually but just at this moment in the wood, I had become aware of it in a much more realistic meaningful way.

I have always had the obstacle in feeling that I must be this body, since else I would not have the benefit of these sensory organs, the mind, and the intellect and so the experience of this phenomenal world – via the perceptual field. It disappears when I close my eyes when I am asleep. When so, it is replaced by a dreaming perceptual field and in the case of deep sleep there is a complete lack of awareness. Yet I am still alive and wake up again into the day-to-day perceptual world.

The difficulty arises in that I am sure that when I am dead, I will no longer have the body and so the benefit of the sensory organs etc. i.e., the means to be aware of anything in the perceptual field. Yet today i.e., in the woods. I felt it is really true that I, the Self have nothing to do with the body, the sensory organs, this phenomenal world and so on.

Presumably (I imagine) dying is like waking up in the absolute sense and realising that I simply am. I am consciousness itself; I am consciousness, eternal, infinite and blissful. What will be changed is that I will no longer be associated with a specific intellect, mind, senses, and a body and so, because I have come to know this in my life through meditation etc. I will never again need to be (born).

I remembered a paragraph in Shankara's Crest - Jewel of Discrimination and I think there is no need for me to worry about the difficulty mentioned above.

"When an illumined soul has attained oneness with Brahman, his body may wither and fall anywhere, like the shrivelled leaf of a tree. What does it matter? For he has already freed himself from body-consciousness, burning it away in the fire of knowledge.

The illumined soul lives eternally conscious of his oneness with Brahman. He tastes continually the joy of the Atman the one without a second. In putting off this garment of skin,

flesh, and bone he does not have to consider if the place, the time, or the circumstances are suitable."
Shankara's Crest Jewel of Discrimination, page 113

13 Grace – the free and unearned favour of God (OUP dictionary). For me, grace also comes indirectly through others who you meet or interact with on your way in space-time e.g. I remember in the days when there were. bus conductors one West Indian bus conductor, in particular who was so cheerful and alive that simply by being on the bus my mood, and I perceived the mood of many others also, was elevated and influenced positively. They must be since I remember it here and now writing about it many years later. Also remember others who may be devotees on the path, they see the 'One' within you much to your benefit (i.e., Grace); as a devotee when out and about intent on seeing the 'one' in the 'many', inevitably you will make progress it's a bit like because of your meditation God comes to the surface, the 'many' therefore receive that benefit (i.e., Grace)

14 Person who has no religion or whose religion is not that of the majority.

(OUP dictionary).

15 Originally from the Arabic for Infidel, racially abusive and offensive term

(OUP dictionary).

16 The Place of Women in Pure Islam 1996 by M. Rafiqul-Haqq and P. Newton
(The purpose of this booklet is to consider the place of women in the pure teaching of Islam. It must be recognised that not every Muslim, nor every Muslim nation follows all of these teachings. These teachings come from both the Qur'an and the Hadith. The Hadith is 'The Tradition of Mohammad', that is, the stories of Mohammad's deeds and sayings.)
The reader can read this for themselves in detail; but you

can get an inkling merely by reading the sub-headings
listed below:

"Women are deficient in intelligence and religion.
Women are deficient in gratitude.
Women are deficient as witnesses.
The woman is a toy.
The woman is 'awrah [latin pudendum(literally) a thing to
be ashamed of]
The woman is like a rib.

Husband's desires must be met at once.
Obedience to the husband is the key to paradise.
Husband's rights are divine.
Husband's rights are greater than the sacrifice of woman's
breasts.

Man may beat and sexually desert his wife.
Men may marry up to four free women and have sex with an
unlimited number of slave girls.
Man's right to divorce his wife.
Man's privileges in the custody of children.
Men in paradise will enjoy sex with perpetually exquisite
virgin women.

The significance of the marriage contract
The significance of the dowry
Man has the right to prevent his wife from caring for her
child from a previous marriage.
Man has the right to refuse his wife's daily maintenance.
Spiritual standing of women."

17 Concerned with power or status within a particular social
    group rather than matters of principle (OUP dictionary).

18 Islam's Sharia law

Is cast from the words of Muhammad, called "hadith," his actions, called "sunnah," and the Quran, which he dictated. The Sharia law itself cannot be altered but its interpretation, called "fiqh," by muftis (Islamic jurists) is given some latitude. As a legal system, the Sharia law is exceptionally broad. While other legal codes regulate public behaviour, Sharia regulates public behaviour, private behaviour, and even private beliefs. Compared to other legal codes, the Sharia law also prioritizes punishment over rehabilitation and favours corporal and capital punishments over incarceration.

Of all legal systems in the world today, the Sharia law is the most intrusive and restrictive, especially against women.

According to the Sharia law:

- Theft is punishable by amputation of the hands (Quran 5:38).
- Criticizing or denying any part of the Quran is punishable by death.
- Criticizing Muhammad or denying that he is a prophet is punishable by death.
- Criticizing or denying Allah is punishable by death.
- A Muslim who becomes a non-Muslim is punishable by death.
- A non-Muslim who leads a Muslim away from Islam is punishable by death.
- A non-Muslim man who marries a Muslim woman is punishable by death.
- A woman or girl who has been raped cannot testify in court against her rapist(s).*
- Testimonies of 4 male witnesses are required to prove rape of a female Quran 24:13).*

*See page 125, "Child of 13 stoned to death in Somalia".

- A woman or girl who alleges rape without producing 4 male witnesses is guilty of adultery.*
- A woman or girl found guilty of adultery is punishable by death (Islamophobia").*
- A male convicted of rape can have his conviction dismissed by marrying his victim.
- Muslim men have sexual rights to any woman/girl not wearing the Hijab (see Taharrush).
- A woman can have 1 husband, who can have up to 4 wives; Muhammad can have more.
- A man can marry an infant girl and consummate the marriage when she is 9 years old.
- Girls' clitoris should be cut (Muhammad's words, *Book 41, Kitab Al-Adab, Hadith 5251*).
- A man can beat his wife for insubordination (see Quran 4:34 and Religion of Peace).
- A man can unilaterally divorce his wife; a wife needs her husband's consent to divorce.
- A divorced wife loses custody of all children over 6 years of age or when they exceed it.
- A woman's testimony in court, allowed in property cases, carries ½ the weight of a man's.
- A female heir inherits half of what a male heir inherits.
- A woman cannot speak alone to a man who is not her husband or relative.
- Meat to eat must be from animals that have been sacrificed to Allah i.e **"Halal."**
- Muslims should engage in **Taqiyya** and lie to non-Muslims to advance Islam.

www.billionbibles.org/sharia/sharia-law.html

Child of 13 stoned to death in Somalia**

October 31, 2008

A girl stoned to death in Somalia this week was 13 years old, not 23, contrary to earlier news reports. She had been accused of adultery in breach of Islamic law.

Aisha Ibrahim Duhulow was killed on Monday 27 October, by a group of 50 men in a stadium in the southern port of Kismayu, in front of around 1,000 spectators. Somali journalists who had reported she was 23 have told Amnesty International that they judged her age by her physical appearance.

Inside the stadium, militia members opened fire when some of the witnesses to the killing attempted to save her life and shot dead a boy who was a bystander. An al-Shabab spokesperson was later reported to have apologized for the death of the child and said the militia member would be punished.

At one point during the stoning, Amnesty International has been told by numerous eyewitnesses that nurses were instructed to check whether Aisha Ibrahim Duhulow was still alive when buried in the ground. They removed her from the ground, declared that she was, and she was replaced in the hole where she had been buried for the stoning to continue.

Aisha Ibrahim Duhulow was accused of adultery, but sources told Amnesty International that she had in fact been raped by three men, and had attempted to report this rape to the al-Shabab militia who control Kismayo. It was this act that resulted in her being accused of adultery and detained. None of men she accused of rape were arrested.

She was detained by militia of the Kismayo authorities, a coalition of Al-shabab and clan militias. During this time, she was reportedly extremely distressed, with some individuals stating she had become mentally unstable.

Amnesty International has campaigned to end the use of the punishment of stoning, calling it gruesome and horrific. This killing of Aisha Ibrahim Duhulow demonstrates the cruelty and the inherent discrimination against women of this punishment.

**See page 126, "How to stone according to the rules".

How to stone according to the rules

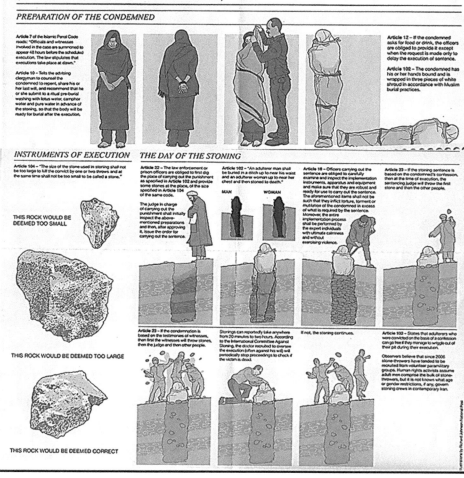

Amnesty International IK 01/Nov/2008
Report and Poster

19 "At the core of the Perennial Philosophy are 4 fundamental doctrines.

1. **First**: The phenomenal world of matter and of individualized consciousness – the world of things and animals and men and gods – is the manifestation of a Divine Ground within which all partial realities have their being, and apart from which they would be non-existent.

2. **Second**: Human beings are capable not merely of knowing about the Divine Ground by inference; they can also realize its existence by a direct intuition, superior to discursive reasoning. This immediate knowledge unites the knower with that which is known.

3. **Third**: Man possesses a double nature, a phenomenal ego, and an eternal Self, which is the inner man, the spirit, the spark of divinity within the soul. It is possible for a man, if he so desires, to identify himself with the spirit and therefore with the Divine Ground, which is of the same or like nature with the spirit.

4. **Fourth**: Man's life on earth has only one end and purpose: to identify himself with his eternal Self and so to come to unitive knowledge of the Divine Ground."

Bhagavad Gita Introduction by
Aldous Huxley page 7

20 Literally action, whether bodily, linguistic, or mental. The unseen potentials for future pain and pleasure, which we accumulate as the result of good or bad action.

(The Oxford Companion to Philosophy
2nd edition OUP).

21 As per Sheldon three physical components and closely related psychological components, physically these are endomorphy (at extreme end soft, rounded and easily may become grossly fat). mesomorphy (at extreme end, hard, big-boned, and strong muscled); ectomorph (at

extreme end slender, small bones and stringy, weak, unemphatic muscles).

Psychologically
Endomorph (is Viscerotonia - at extreme end love of food, and of eating, love of comfort and luxury, love of ceremoniousness, indiscriminate amiability and love of people as such, fear of solitude and craving for company, uninhibited expression of emotion, love of childhood, in the form of an intense enjoyment of family life, craving for affection and social support and the need for people when in trouble).
Mesomorphy (is Somatotonia – at extreme end the dominating traits are love of muscular activity, aggressiveness and lust for power, indifference to pain, callousness in regard to other people's feelings, a love of combat and competitiveness, a high degree of physical courage, a nostalgic feeling, not for childhood, but for youth, the period of maximum muscular power, a need for activity when in trouble).
Ectomorphic (is Cerebrotonic- at extreme end is over-alert, over-sensitive introvert, who is more concerned with what goes on behind the eyes – with the constructions of thought and imagination, with the variations of feeling and consciousness – than with the external world, to which, in their different ways, the viscerotonic and the somatotonic pay their primary attention and allegiance. Cerebrotonics have little or no desire to dominate, nor do they feel the viscerotonic's indiscriminate liking for people as people, on the contrary they want to live and let live, and their passion for privacy is intense. Solitary confinement the most terrible punishment that can be inflicted on the soft, round, genial person is for the cerebrotonic, no punishment at all. For him the ultimate horror is the boarding school and the barracks. In company cerebrotonics are nervous and shy, tensely inhibited and unpredictably moody. (It is a significant fact that no extreme cerebrotonic has ever been a good actor or actress). Cerebrotonics hate to slam

doors or raise their voices and suffer acutely from the unrestrained bellowing and trampling of the somotonic. Their manner is restrained and when it comes to expressing their feelings they are extremely reserved. The emotional gush of the viscerotonic strikes them as offensively shallow and even insincere, nor have they any patience with viscerotonic ceremoniousness, and love of luxury and magnificence...)

Extracted (I have forced myself not to continue on) from 'The Perennial Philosophy' by Aldous Huxley
1980 Chatto & Windus Ltd

22 Think carefully about; focus one's mind for spiritual purposes (OUP dictionary).

23 Whenever I hear the mention of the nature and nurture debate, I am reminded of the parable, included here: (it is probably a total misunderstanding by me, however that's my interpretation).
"And a great crowd coming together and those in each city coming to him, he spoke by a parable: A sower went out to sow his seed: and as he sowed, some fell by the wayside; and it was trampled down, and the birds of the air devoured it. And some fell on rock; and as soon as it sprang up, it withered away, because it lacked moisture. And some fell among thorns, and the thorns sprang up with it and choked it. And others fell on good ground, and sprang up, and bear fruit a hundredfold. And when he had said these things, he cried, he who has ears to hear let him hear!" - Jesus
Luke 8:4-8,

24 Concerned with principles of right and wrong behaviour (OUP dictionary) e.g., virtuous, good, righteous, upright, upstanding, high-minded, principled, honourable, honest, just, noble, incorruptible, scrupulous, respectable, decent, clean-living, law-abiding.

25 The term 'within' like the term 'in' doesn't mean that the reality is inside or contained by the part, it is like the

reference earlier to the 'screen' and the 'film-show', i.e., within but beyond, pervades but has no contact.

26   Item 1: from the Mandukya Upanishad, translated by: Sri Purohit Swami and W.B. Yeats (1937) and Item 2: Mandukya Upanishad, translated by Juan Mascaró (1965).

27   See bibliography re books marked with an * (re Perception)

28   There was a study done at Oak Ridge Lab. by Paul C. Aebersold in 1953 that found that 98 percent of all the atoms in a person's body change out every year, and that within five years all the atoms had changed.

Time Magazine

29   'Crest Jewel of Discrimination', Introduction by Swami Prabhavananda & Christopher Isherwood page 22

30   Brahman (the absolute) and Atman (the absolute present in the individual) are one and the same.

31   Two of these numbers relate to the basic force e.g., one of these defines how firmly atomic nuclei bind together and how all atoms on earth were made. Its value controls the power from the Sun and, more sensitively, how stars transmute hydrogen into all the atoms of the periodic table, this number ϵ has the value 0.007, if ϵ were 0.006 or 0.008, we could not exist". Of the other numbers, two fix the size and overall 'texture' of our universe and determine whether it will continue forever; and two more fix the properties of space itself.

Martin Rees
'Just six numbers – that Shape the Universee ...'

32   While looking for a good description of 'anthropy' I came across this quotation by Ralph Estling from the New Scientist. This makes the point much more powerfully:

"Underlying the argument for the supernatural or the super-intelligent is the anthropic principle, the realisation that the Universe is so exactly the right kind of Universe for man that we must meditate on the thousands of coincidences that are absolutely essential for man, or indeed, life to exist. One slight variation in just one of those thousands of essential coincidences would have altered the physical Universe drastically, possibly totally. Yet, down to the fine structure constants that dictate gravitational, electromagnetic, and strong and weak nuclear forces, and up to basic biological prerequisites, we find the cosmos in general, our Sun in particular, and Earth most particularly, so minutely attuned to us, that the conclusion seems inescapable: God or someone else of the same name made it like that, with us in mind. It is, we insist, just too much of a coincidence, just too much of a miracle, to say it is pure, unnecessitated chance."

(cited in 'Superforce: The search for a Grand Unified Theory of Nature'. by Paul Davies – Heinemann page 238).

33 Hydrogen, the major component of the universe, is composed of a proton and electron only, however I am only concerned with the essence I am a devotee not a scientist, this pattern works for me.

34 It is the 'idea' or pattern that concerns me even though this may be more mystical than scientific, e.g., the electron is said not to truly exist in space and time but only emerges into momentary actual existence by the act of measurement.

35 "During the 'night of Brahma', the phase of potentiality, these gunas are in a state of perfect equilibrium, and Prakriti (Maya) remains undifferentiated. Creation is the disturbance of this equilibrium. The gunas then begin to enter into a vast variety of combinations, corresponding to the various forms of differentiated mind and matter. Their characteristics may be known from their products in the psychic and physical worlds.

In the physical world, sattwa embodies all that is pure and fine, rajas embodies the active principle and tamas the principle of solidity and resistance. All three are present in everything, but one guna always predominates. For example, sattwa predominates in sunlight, rajas in an erupting volcano, and tamas in a block of granite.

The gunas also represent the different stages in the evolution in any particular entity. Sattwa is the essence of the form to be realized; tamas is the inherent obstacle to its realization; and rajas is the power by which that obstacle is removed, and the essential form becomes manifest.

In the mind of man, sattwa expresses itself psychologically as tranquillity, purity and calmness; rajas as passion, restlessness, aggressive activity; tamas as stupidity, laziness, and inertia. Sometimes one guna is predominant; sometimes another; and a man's mood and character vary accordingly. But man can cultivate any one of the gunas, by his actions and thoughts and way of living. We are taught that tamas can be overcome by the cultivation of rajas, and rajas by the cultivation of sattwa. However, the ultimate ideal is to transcend sattwa also and reach the Atman, which is above and beyond the gunas."

Aldous Huxley Bhagavad-Gita page 178.

36 The reading brain can be likened to the real-time collaborative effort of a symphony orchestra, with various parts of the brain working together, like sections of instruments, to maximise our ability to decode the written text in front of us:

- The temporal lobe is responsible for phonological awareness and decoding/discriminating sounds.
- The frontal lobe handles speech production, reading fluency, grammatical usage, and comprehension, making it possible to understand simple and complex grammar in our native language.
- The angular and supramarginal gyrus serve as a "reading integrator" a conductor of sorts, linking the

different parts of the brain together to execute the action of reading. These areas of the brain connect the letters c, a, and t to the word cat that we can then read aloud.

www.scilearn.com/the-reading-brain/

37 Bypassing the fact that a letter is itself a relationship of parts, i.e., curves, and straight lines at various angles.

38 It is true that it is rather an arbitrary place to start since the proton and the neutron each consist of a relationship of 3 smaller parts called quarks. The proton consists of 2 up-quarks and 1 down-quark; the neutron consists of 2 down-quarks and 1 up-quark. There exist a range of other sub-particles, e.g., other quarks of types: charm, strange, top & bottom, and other particles e.g., the muon and the tau, not to mention anti-particles. It is said however, "That everything you see in the terrestrial world and the heavens above appears to be made from a combination of electrons, up-quarks, and down-quarks. No experimental evidence indicates that any of these three particles is built up from something smaller"

'The Elegant Universe – Superstrings, Hidden dimensions, and the quest for the Ultimate Theory Brian Greene

39 See "In search of Schrödinger's Cat: Quantum Physics and Reality", John Gribbin A Black Swan Book 0-552-12555-5

40 In his posthumously published book, 'The Phenomenon of Man', Teilhard writes of the unfolding of the material cosmos, from primordial particles to the development of life, human beings and the noosphere, and finally to his vision of the Omega Point in the future, which is 'pulling' all creation towards it. He was a leading proponent of orthogenesis, the idea that evolution occurs in a directional, goal driven way, argued in terms that today go under the banner of convergent evolution. Teilhard

argued in Darwinian terms with respect to biology, and supported the synthetic model of evolution, but argued in Lamarckian terms for the development of culture, primarily through the vehicle of education. (Wikipedia. Org/wiki/Pierre_Teilhard_de_Chardin accessed 30 April 2011).

41 The parts in their totality (all atoms, visible & invisible) comprise only a little more than 4.5% of what is, the rest is dark energy 70%, dark matter 25 % and the left over (0.5%) is light radiations and neutrinos – see The Cosmic Density Pyramid page 115 "The view from the centre of the universe".

> Joel Primack & Nancy Ellen Abrams, ISBN: 978-0-00-719352-3

42 Our planet and we are inextricably linked to the stars because stars have changed hydrogen and helium into all the heavier elements we are made of. Stars begin as vast clouds of gas, mostly hydrogen and helium. Light as those individual atoms are, there are so many of them that together their gravity is immense, and it gradually compresses the clouds until there is so much pressure and heat at the centre that atomic nuclei fuse together. The energy released by this nuclear process - which is a continuous hydrogen bomb - ignites the cloud and a star is born.

A tiny fraction of the hydrogen and helium in galaxies is in giant gas planets like Jupiter; some is still floating as clouds that glow only if they are heated and lit up by nearby stars; but the majority of all visible matter in the universe is hydrogen and helium now shining in the form of stars. Stars manufacture the other elements but not all in the same way.

There are a few super-massive stars, many more middle-sized ones like our sun, and great numbers of faint stars about a third the mass of our sun. The faint small ones don't produce many heavy atoms, but the mid-to-large ones do, each in its own way producing different essential elements. It is huge stars more than about eight times the mass of the sun that produce most of the oxygen and neon and all of the really heavy elements.

After such mega-stars with their immense gravity crush and fuse the hydrogen nuclei in their cores, their outer layers swell, and they become red giant stars. As such stars evolve further, their centres develop an onion like structure, with hydrogen fusing in an outer layer, helium in a deeper layer, then carbon, neon, oxygen, with silicon and sulphur fusing in the core. Eventually the core becomes mostly iron, the most tightly bound nucleus, and then further fusion is impossible. But gravity never stops.

The intense gravity of the outer layers of the star still pressing down on the iron core of the star causes the structure of the atomic nuclei themselves in the core to collapse, and the star ends up as one or the other of the two densest things in the universe: a neutron star or a black hole. About 99% of the energy of the collapse is carried off by a brief burst of particles called neutrinos. The neutrinos can escape from the dense collapsing core of the star in only a few seconds since they have no electrical charge and interact only weakly; they also have only very tiny masses. It is the remaining 1% of the energy that produces the visible explosion and seeds the nearby universe with heavy atoms.

The very heaviest elements like gold and uranium are apparently produced during the supernova explosion itself. Fifty times per second, a supernova occurs in some galaxy in the visible universe, spewing out into space enormous quantities of heavy elements that may travel millions of light-years before falling into the gravitational field of some newly forming solar system. Those heavy elements may join together to create in that new solar system a planet that billions of years later will pulse with life.

But not all the heavy atoms are made in such supernovas. Medium-sized stars more massive than our sun produced the medium-weight atoms like carbon and nitrogen that make up more than 20% of the weight of your body. Here's how: after millions of years of fusing hydrogen to make helium in their cores, those stars used up the hydrogen and started fusing helium to make carbon and oxygen in their cores, and they too (like the giant stars) swelled up and became red giant stars. Later the red giant evolved into an even larger "asymptotic red giant", and then blew off its outer layers to form a gas cloud called a planetary nebula. This eventually dispersed into space, leaving behind a tiny remnant called a white dwarf, which typically has half the mass of the sun compressed to the size of the earth. A teaspoon of white dwarf would have a mass of several tons.

The carbon atoms in our bodies mostly came from planetary nebulas. Planetary nebulas from stars that started out a little more massive than the sun also contain a lot of nitrogen, which is the main constituent of the air we breathe ....

Joel Primack and Nancy Ellen Abrams – The View from the Centre of the Universe. Page 96 – 98

43   You need to develop even vision i.e., God is 'One' within the perceptual field just like the screen is 'One' within the ever-changing film-show.

On walking out today I realised that each view (of the perceptual field) is unique and will never be seen again. This person who is passing me in the street, the sound and sight of this lorry passing and everything else which is seen, heard, felt and so on is the experience 'Now'. but then replaced immediately by the next 'Now'. That which remains 'unchanged' amidst this perceptual field is the 'Self' (the screen, the eternal witness).

Today, whilst walking towards Collier Row and stopping on the small bridge to look down at the river 'Rom' (hence 'Romford'). I am struck, as I have often been, that the perception of the river is unchanging, I see it as just one thing and motionless. The water flows rapidly and there are eddies and swirls where the depth is narrowed because of irregularities on its bed and the flow is accompanied by nonstop sound.

It seems you cannot, in a sense, see the water (other than it being one thing – the river) water comes into the point you are looking at but immediately it is replaced by the water following it. The water swirls and eddies the same, so although (you know) the water is flowing, and it seems that you can see it however, in fact you cannot. It comes into consciousness and leaves consciousness continuously and before you can see it, it has gone, this is the same with the celluloid frames on the roll of film, you cannot perceive an individual frame which when seen is static, a snapshot and unchanging. The frames move along too quickly to be seen yet give the sense of a reality, seeing its continuously changing flow.

Much of the sense-data is screened out, otherwise we could not deal with the sheer volume and intensity that arrives continuously to our senses e.g., this can give the problem of 'perceptual overload' that can be and is often experienced by the patient coming around in the Intensive Care Unit (ICU] following an operation say, a Coronary Artery Bypass Graft (CABG).

A distorted view of the nurse coming in and out of view, the bright lights and the continuous bleeping and blinking and noises of alarms going of, which happens normally and can become much more intense when there is say a cardiac arrest in the bay opposite or adjacent. Above all the presence of the Endotracheal Tube (ET) tube in the throat and the many drips and drainage tubes the patient is connected to, also the effects of drugs in the system and the continuous presence of the nurse who is milking the drains, taking the observations, and trying to comfort and communicate with the patient as he gradually warms up and becomes more conscious. The above situation is what can happen in the extreme situation outside of the normal routine, also the same kind of thing can happen in an opposite sense when there is a 'perceptual deprivation' more common with the elderly patient placed in a side bay and so prone to suffer from the 'white wall syndrome'. This is due to a lack of stimulation and being left alone in a strange environment.

It can lead to such a patient becoming confused or disturbed.

Then it occurs to me while standing on the bridge over the river Rom, that 'everything' i.e., the never-ending flow of sense-data which makes up the perceptual field behaves in the same way.

In the same way, as above described, one set of sense-data is immediately replaced by the next set of sense-data. I am aware of this when I see a view (a van turning into the road just in front of me, the tree in partial view in the right-hand section of my visual field, the leaves trembling in the breeze, the flash of reflected sunlight in the rear window of the van and myriad other events at that moment coming together to give just that 'one' view. Which is 'here' and then 'gone' immediately to be replaced by the next view. Each view will never be seen again although of course we are not aware of this, rather like the roll of the film, being just a series of frames, each frame is still and motionless, but it is replaced by the next slide so quickly that we don't see the join and it gives us the perception of the events proceeding seamlessly.

Sense-data continuously arrives at the sensory organs (eyes, ears etc.) to be transformed into neurological impulses and conveyed to the relevant areas of the brain where it is related together, where the dots are joined so to speak. The resultant created imaging is then projected back to give us our perception of what we take to be the reality, see the diagrams a, b & c.

(a) One view is of a beautiful girl but then the way the dots can be joined can switch and what is seen is the face of an old hag.

(b) The dog with his nose to the ground is a famous example of closure. When you see the dog, it suddenly becomes solid. A gestalt is formed. Your perceptual system succeeds in connecting the dots, so to speak, and you perceive an object.

(c) Shows a profile which can be two faces or a candle holder and again you can switch from one to the other. There is perhaps not enough sense-data to determine a correct creation of what the true perceptual reality is.

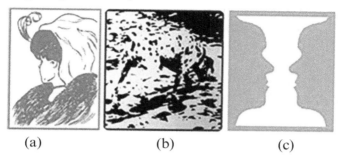

(a)   (b)   (c)

These images and others can be found on the web e.g., search for 'the rotating mask illusion' and you will see how your interpretation switches from one view to the other – what is 'real?'.

I was reminded of the passage in the book 'Siddartha', and it was probably that which led me inwardly to stop and look at the river Rom.

"But today he only saw one of the river's secrets, one that gripped his soul. He saw that the water continually flowed and yet it was always there; it was always the same and yet every moment it was new."

He once asked him, 'Have you also learned that secret from the river; that there is no such thing as time?'

A bright smile spread over Vaseduva's face.

'Yes, Siddhartha,' he said. 'Is this what you mean? That the river is everywhere at the same time, at the source and at the mouth, at the waterfall, at the ferry, at the current, in the ocean and in the mountains, everywhere, and that the present only exists for it, not the shadow of the past, nor the shadow of the future?'

'That is, it,' said Siddhartha, 'and when I learned that I reviewed my life and it was also a river, and Siddhartha the boy, Siddhartha the mature man and Siddhartha the old man were only separated by shadows, not through reality. Siddhartha's previous lives were also not in the past, and his death and his return to Brahma are not in the future. Nothing was, nothing will be, everything has

reality and presence.' Siddhartha spoke with delight.
This discovery had made him very happy. Was then not
all sorrow in time, all self-torment and fear in time?
Were not all difficulties and evil in the world conquered
as soon as one conquered time, as soon as one dispelled
time?"

Hermann Hesse. Siddhartha (Picador- Pan Books,
London 1973, page 85

I am not constantly in the state of unity, I am aware of
this and know everything (re the Here and Now)
intellectually and that I should return to that state.

But I am subjected again and again, drawn, and
attracted to the old way of thinking and again feel the
desires and the wish to give in to them, the feelings are
still present, and I find myself dwelling on them as I
have so often done before.

Then having stopped thinking about it, or looking
for it, I suddenly look out of the window to see it is
still snowing and accept (after a trial walking earlier)
that I should give up the practice of going out for a
walk until tomorrow (the first time in nearly a year)
this not because it is snowing (hardly worth bothering
about since it is so slight) or because it is cold but
because it is icy on the pavement under the snow and
it would be foolish.

I would not feel confident at being able to forget
about the risk of slipping up, falling over and so on. I
would not be able to enter unity simply because my
attention would be so much diverted to walking
safely.

Looking out the window and seeing the snow
swirling and dancing I suddenly became aware that I
was 'not looking', I was 'not seeing' - there was no 'I'.
Rather it is that the trees and bushes are where they
are, and the snow is falling and that the window is
where it is, and this body is where it is, and the eyes
are where they are also.

It is just that all these 'objects of perception' as

interpreted (dots joined up) by the 'organs of perception' are superimposed on the 'Self' (which is everywhere and nowhere) which simply 'Is'.

As I have often said and written previously; it is a question of identification. The sense of 'I' arises because the 'Self' is identified with this body and identified me as an individual as in this place; looking out the window; seeing with my eyes; that the snow is falling, that the snow is the other side of this window and so on.

However, at that instant I was aware that I was 'not looking' but instead I was aware of simply 'Being', of simply 'Isness' - that I was the 'Whole' within these 'relationships of parts', greater than the sum total of them yet distinct.

44 Capital S to indicate the real self. Remember God is God. You don't become God you only remove the false identification and then realize God is.

45 *"Subtler than the subtlest, greater than the greatest" – Svetasvatara Upanishad, 'The Upanishads' translated by Swami Prabahavananda & Frederick Manchester.*

46 "**Karma** Yoga, as its name implies, is concerned with work and action. By working selflessly for our neighbours, by regarding all action as a sacramental offering to God, by doing our duty without anxiety or concern for success or failure, praise, or blame, we can gradually annihilate the ego-idea. Through Karma we can transcend Karma and experience the Reality, which is beyond all action.

Bhakti is the Yoga of devotion – devotion to Iswara, the Personal God, or to a great teacher, a Christ, a Buddha, a Ramakrishna. Through this personal devotion, this loving service to an embodied ideal, the devotee will ultimately transcend personality altogether. This is the Yoga of ritual, of worship, of the religious sacraments.

Ritual plays an important part in it, as a physical aid to concentration – for the acts of ritual, like the acts of Karma Yoga, bring the mind back repeatedly from its distractions and help to keep it steadily upon its object. For many the easiest path.

Jnana Yoga is more suited to those who mistrust the emotional fervour of worship. It is the Yoga of pure discrimination. It transcends the intellect through the intellect. It needs no Iswara, no alter, no image, no ritual. It seeks a more immediate approach to the Impersonal Brahman. This path may be more direct, but it is also hard.

Raja Yoga – the Yoga of meditation – combines, to some extent, the three others. It does not exclude Karma Yoga, and it makes use both of the Bhakti and the Jnana approach – since true meditation is a blend of the devotional and the discriminative.

Aldous Huxley from "Shankara's Crest-Jewel of Discrimination" page 32

47 Refers to any device that converts acoustic waves in air to electrical signals for transmission, recording and reproduction, the use of carbon granules in microphones is now probably obsolete.

48 94.9 Megahertz or 94.9 million cycles per second.

49 Referred to as 'frequency modulation' (FM) – a means of broadcasting an audio signal by radio; the audio signals say vibrations between 20 Hz and 17KHz generated by the human voice and the musical instruments are superimposed onto the carrier frequency, say 94.9 MHz.

50 The carrier frequency is removed or subtracted, and the result is that the audio signal remains as the difference.

51 Stephen Hawking wrote in a 'A Brief History of Time' that even if we had TOE, it would necessarily be a set of equations. He wrote *"What is it that breathes fire into the equations and makes a universe for them to describe?'*
En.wikipedia.org/wiki/Theory_of_Everything accessed 30 April 2011.

52 The European Space Agency's Planck satellite has released the most detailed map of the universe ever created refining estimates of the age of the universe and its composition, as well as showing some interesting anomalies that scientists can't yet explain.

   The new map made of the first trillionth of a trillionth of a second after Big Bang.

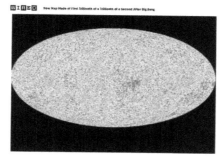

53 Sync i.e., synchronize – cause to occur or operate at the same time or rate e.g., as in synchronized swimming.

54 *"Beware of false prophets, who come to you in sheep's clothing but inwardly are ravenous wolves. You will recognize them by their fruits. Are grapes gathered from thorn bushes, or figs from thistles? So, every healthy tree bears good fruit, but the diseased tree bears bad fruit. A healthy tree cannot bear bad fruit, nor can a diseased tree bear good fruit. Every tree that does not bear good fruit is cut down and thrown into the fire. Thus, you will recognize them by their fruits".*

Matthew 7: 1 - 29

55 The point of including these notes is to reiterate that as
    time goes by the fact that the Holocaust and such events
    actually happened seems to be getting lost. I recall when I
    was young and finding out about this that I found it hard
    to believe that human beings could descend to such
    depths (incidentally from the people who gave the world
    'Bach').

    Now these days, it seems the same sort of disbelief is
    present for many people because perhaps these events are
    passing into history and disturbingly many people now
    seem to know nothing about it or don't believe, or think,
    that it has all been exaggerated.

    For many, as previously mentioned, it is argued that
    the fact that the Holocaust actually happened shows there
    is no God, and of course there are many, many other
    examples which people cite to show that there is no God.

    For me however, it strengthens my determination to get
    out and about walking and meditating. I accept
    completely that God does not do anything, like the screen
    upon which the film-show plays out does not do anything.
    The depths that human beings descend too only makes it
    more important to keep going and so eventually to reveal
    this screen.

    I can imagine what it must have been like for the people
    arriving at Auschwitz; when they disembarked from the
    cramped train wagons, having not been able to sit or lie
    down; having had nothing to eat or drink or adequate
    toilet facilities over a journey lasting possibly several days
    in the stifling heat of summer or the freezing cold of
    winter, of stop and start progress towards who knows
    where?

    Then the blast of fresh air when the doors were slid
    open, and they were ordered out onto the platform to be
    shepherded by the Guards and their barking dogs
    towards the SS officer who separated out the woman and
    children from their fathers; husbands from their wives;
    mothers from their children indicating them to go to the
    left or to the right.

    The men and those fit for work directed towards the

camp. The women, children, and the elderly or those unfit directed to the shower building, there to undress and fold their clothes etc., only then for the doors to be closed and sealed before the gas was delivered from the roof openings (not water for a shower after all).

Following a delay for the gassing to have taken effect the bodies then removed and fed into the ovens.

It was reported by a witness at the Nuremberg Trials that on one occasion from the camp she heard much screaming and later was told that on this occasion the gas had run out and was inadequate to kill everyone, that consequently the prisoners doing the work of clearing the bodies had to throw the children into the furnace while they were still alive. It is not surprising in these circumstances that a person would think 'there is no God'.

It's possible there may have been the odd person here and there who were caught up in this nightmare (by virtue of being classified as Jewish, others also e.g., gypsies but the principle rationale being primarily destruction of the Jews ' The Final Solution') and yet through it all may have been able to keep their focus on God (the 'screen' within) and I expect for those around them there was some inner strength and comfort experienced by being in their company.

However, I cannot say anything meaningful about this since I was blessed by having been born and socialised in England. I am classified as 'C of E' and was not indoctrinated or groomed. I only read about the matters mentioned above (that took place mostly before my birth in 1944). At that time when reading about it, I found it hard to take in, or indeed to believe that all of this really did happen.

It must be true that ordinary people lived in proximity to the ghetto and the camp, that they could see, hear, and smell what was going on, and it must be true they cooperated and went along with it, moved into the empty Jewish houses, drove the trains, worked the signals and so on.

I am aware that I am not brave or physically impressive and wondered how I would have stood up against these sorts of human beings or resisted being indoctrinated or taken in by their propaganda, or how easily I would have succumbed to the peer pressure and the socialising process during this Nazi period.

I was motivated to strive through meditation to reveal the screen because of such examples.

I remember a scene in the film 'Ben Hur' which I saw when it was released (1959), it made a big impression on me, far more powerful than the film as a whole re the chariot race and so on. I bought the DVD again (November 2020), in order to find the scene again and thus more accurately describe it. This in case others might want to look for it and see if it has the same effect on them.

The scene happens after Ben Hur has been sentenced and is being driven along on foot (chained together with others) across the desert. The party reaches a place where there is water, and the group is stopped so that the guards and horses can drink. Ordinary people out of compassion take water to the prisoners so they can have a drink also. The guard has been instructed beforehand that Ben Hur is not to be given any water.

The group on reaching the oasis had passed a carpenters workshop and although you only see the carpenter's back you realise later on that this is 'Jesus'. Ben Hur having had water offered to him by one of the ordinary people had this snatched away by the guard, and it can be seen this brings him to the end of his tether and he collapses, seemingly destroyed and broken. Then you see the hands of this carpenter support Ben Hur's head and giving him water to drink from the gourd. The guard seeing this shouts out "I said no water for him" and starts to approach wielding the whip obviously to stop the carpenter but the carpenter looks up into the face of the guard.

The guard stops in his tracks and recoils as it were with a look of bewilderment and shock on his face, he is confused and shamed, and he backs of. Ben Hur after having drunk the water looks up at Jesus's face with gratitude but then this changes to a look of wonder and although the guard sets the group going again on their way, Ben Hur keeps looking back at Jesus and his demeanour and poise is restored.

It is obvious that he, and also the guard, have looked into the face of Jesus and have come face to face with Reality as though they had looked into a calm, pure, pond of water and had the realisation that it is their Self.

It comes across that Ben Hur is restored and that he will come through everything now he has this inner knowledge. Whereas the guard who has also realised he has seen the 'Self' is painfully aware and uncomfortable with how he measures up against this Self.

Some years ago (approx. 50 years ago) I was making progress and had come across 'The Bhagavad Gita' things were going well but this was, as it were, when the sun was shining. I was living in London and had just started my first settled employment (as a Delivery Postman, since leaving the Army 3 or 4 years earlier).

I was not being tested since, as I have said, I was now a civilian in London. It was easy to be diverted by the many distractions.

On a visit to an ex-Army friend who lived in Dublin. (This was 1972). I went on the train up to Belfast; it was like I imagine being in the blitz. Stepping from the train onto the platform it was obviously a war zone, the Europa hotel directly outside had its windows boarded up (being a Hotel of note it had to have its windows reglazed over and over again due to frequent bomb blast damage) It occurred to me that if you were in the business of securing premises with shattered windows and then re-glazing them you would soon become a millionaire.

The first impression of Belfast was very powerful because the whole area around was like it had been bombed and flattened. Later I found out that this was largely due to the construction of a major development i.e. a road or dual carriageway coming right through this area of Belfast.

While walking around I was passed by Army patrols, on foot and in land rovers. I felt a strong pull of camaraderie (having not long left the Army myself) and I felt that this is where I should be.

In Belfast at this time, I felt I would not be distracted, and the situation would help me to concentrate (it is said that knowing you will be hanged the next day really concentrates the mind although of course I was not under such a sentence of death, but it could happen at any time that I might be in the same place as a bomb which went off) so if I was here then I would meditate and keep it up in an undistracted way.

In the Post Office it is acceptable to transfer to another place and then simply report to the Post Office and work in that new place.

I asked for this transfer (from SWDO Victoria SW1 to Belfast Royal Avenue) and it was agreed with the proviso that I had to first fix myself up with a place to live over there and then the transfer could take place.

To be brief I moved to Belfast around March 1973.

I had found a place to live in the University area which was relatively neutral and safe, and I started work and my first walk was in this same area i.e., in streets branching off the Ormeau Road.

In the Post Office it was the practice that a Catholic postman would not be asked to deliver in a Loyalist/Protestant area and vice versa e.g., when a postman goes off sick or on holiday someone else has to step in to take on his walk. The postman when asked if he could take on the 'Walk' would simply say No, and this would be accepted by the line manager without any argument.

It must be explained that there were Republic/Catholic areas and Loyalist/Protestant areas e.g. The Shankill Road is Loyalist and running roughly parallel is the Falls Road and any side streets which lead from one to the other are walled off at the central point (this side of the wall is Shankill the other side is the Falls). I think its true to say that some people on the Shankill side had never in their life gone into the Falls side literally a few feet away on the other side of the wall and vice versa.

It was also the practice that you never asked anyone where they lived since this marked you out immediately as Loyalist or Nationalist ('Us or Them' so to speak).

After a while I found somewhere else to live, this was in a side street 'Thorndale Avenue' parallel to Antrim Road, from my window I could see the turning into New Lodge Road - a very heavily Catholic area.

When I finished my walk (still working in the University area) I used to go to a café and I was off my guard when someone asked me where I lived and without thinking I mentioned the street and the next thing I knew I was hit in the face and bleeding so heavily it wouldn't stop, I ended up in hospital and in fact I was kept in overnight, this because when I was fit to be discharged it was about 9 pm and the stop overnight was for safety reasons.

At the time I was there Belfast was quite a dangerous place and the seriousness of it was soon apparent. Being a Postman was also a bit like being on the front line, one day I was walking up one of the main roads, probably the Falls road because the road in front went to the left, and before I reached this turning, I heard bursts of machine gun fire.

I stopped and turned back not at all tempted by curiosity to go forward and see what had happened. Later when it was reported it turned out to be two postman walking on the pavement when a vehicle pulled up and (the occupants i.e., loyalists, I assume, shot them dead).

Another example was the murder of some soldiers who were operating incognito working as employees in a commercial laundry service. Out and about in vans collecting and delivering laundry at the same time picking up local information in the areas which otherwise were no-go for to them to visit other than on patrol.

One of the insane, mind bending, incidents which happened while I was there took place, I think, in the tea hut, (I forget the exact details) on a building site on the

Shore road. The people who entered the site said to everyone that they should step out if they were Protestant.

What does one do?

If you stepped forward, then the people with the guns could shoot those that did not step forward because they were Catholics alternatively, they might shoot the people who stepped forward because they were Protestants.

Being neither in one tribe or the other I used to be asked on occasion to do the sensitive walks e.g., where two areas met as in Duncairn Gardens where one side bordered a Protestant area (I was told) and the other bordered a Republican (the New Lodge Road) area. I learned quickly not to speak at all, if possible, this so no one would know I was English, especially relevant if delivering the post in the New Lodge road and surrounding area.

When going to work it was the sensible practice to always vary your route and not get into the routine of going the same way and at the same time.

Delivering post was also a bit difficult since letter boxes were often sealed (to prevent anyone pushing an explosive package through) usually you had to slide post under the door or knock to get someone to come to collect it.

When working inside the sorting office one time I was working at the bottom of the slide where postal bags arriving from the England via the Larne ferry would be offloaded and sent down the chute to us. Our job was to open them and move them to the appropriate destination floor area. I opened one bag and holding the bag open to look in I saw wires which immediately I took to be a bomb. The floor and the building was cleared, this sort of thing i.e., evacuating buildings was not unusual, and it was very efficiently carried out in the same way as though it was a normal fire alarm practice.

Soldiers from Bomb Disposal soon arrived and dealt with the situation. The van which collected the bags offloaded from the ferry at Larne was held up on its journey then one of the post bags was opened the bomb put in then the bag sealed up again. The driver then told to carry on as normal, he would do so because they had his family or a relative which would come to harm if he did not do as he was told to follow the usual routine. (I don't know if this was the case on this occasion, but this was the common practice).

Despite all the events taking place due to the troubles Belfast was definitely a place I liked; I liked the Belfast accent and that you were in sight of the countryside all around (walk up one of the roads e.g., the Shankill and look up you can see the hills) you can go by and over the river and to the docks. But most of all for me the streets were terraces of kitchen parlour-like houses with alleyways linking to other streets so established that they looked kind of organic and natural.

My purpose for moving to Belfast was to walk and meditate on the screen upon which everything is superimposed, the situation with its dangers actually helped me keep focused. I took a methodical approach spreading out a city street map so I could plan routes, the screen (God) is equally present to all and everywhere the same. So, in one sense it didn't matter where I went but I took a systematic approach e.g., New Lodge Road and the streets leading off of it then back via Duncairn Gardens and Antrim road. Up Crumlin Road into an area on the right as I remember called Little Britain (although I may have this wrong since I can't find any reference to it currently) but then through here into the 'Ardoyne' a very Republican area. I carried out these walks and was a bit nervous and naïve, but I found it helped in the sense that "nothing concentrates the mind more than the threat of danger!"

When I was looking for somewhere to live (before I moved to Thorndale Avenue) I was given lists of streets from the agent which were empty. This excess of properties was due to the internal migration of people from the areas they were brought up in, sometimes by being forced out by intimidation and in some cases if I remember rightly, by their houses being set alight.

I was shown round a house in one of the streets off the

Crumlin Road, the agent said I could rent it right away and pay only what I wanted to, the same goes for any other house I wanted him to show me. I didn't take up the invitation since it seemed to be asking for trouble being the only occupant in the street.

Also I saw a great deal and learned a lot just by walking around, one time I saw a young boy (I would guess between 10 and 15) on the corner leaning on the wall very relaxed, natural (seemingly without a care in the world) handsome and smiling unselfconsciously then I saw his face change suddenly into a frown with his attempt to look hard and cool - man, I guess he saw someone of his tribe (this was a street in New Lodge Road area so the Republican tribe). It was peer pressure (the 'Them and Us' issue). I got it that he was under pressure and felt that he had to fit in. It was such a disturbing experience and made me aware of the damage the situation the activists or terrorists were responsible for causing.

Such corruption leading probably to that boy growing up to become a good republican hating the loyalists (or a good loyalist hating the republicans since the same socialisation process was taking place in the protestant tribal areas, I am sure).

I had (and still have) no respect for those who committed atrocities for some ideological or political cause. I am uneasy with the word 'Evil' because God alone is real and Evil (also the Devil, Satan etc.) cannot, for me exist, How can such entities be superimposed upon God.

I can see that bad and good has a place but the idea that there is an entity separated from God and an enemy so to speak doesn't make any sense to me. It does have a meaning perhaps to some people brought up on these stories and then referred to in the attempt to frighten them into being good e.g., Satan being an Angel who succumbed to temptation and so on and consequently fell out or was banished from Heaven, however these are stories which have been written into the Bible or scriptures and maybe they have a powerful and good effect.

I know that it is not possible to discuss Absolute Reality (God) in language (God is not IN space-time therefore cannot be described in space-time languages etc. I know also that what I 'Think', what I 'Say' and what I 'Do' takes place in the presence of God,

I also know however that God cannot be harmed, soiled, tainted or whatever; and I realise that I should not keep anything hidden from God. If I commit inappropriate thinking, talking, actions then I no longer have any fear that God will be offended, it is much better to be entirely open to God, I want God to pervade me, my mind, down to its deepest depths. God doesn't do anything; consequences deriving from my inappropriate thinking, talking, actions are dealt with through Karma.

I was at that time unaware of how much that anyone walking down a street stood out as not belonging in that street, that area. This would be monitored by the army and also by the locals who operated a kind of neighbourhood watch.

I found out that the New Lodge area was patrolled by 42 Royal Marine Commando (I think on a 3-year tour) and when walking down a street off the New Lodge Road a couple of Land Rovers would appear with a couple of marines in front and in the back. A patrol would make their own decisions and would decide where to go as they went along, never keeping to a routine. I think I just saw them pass by but the next time I was in the area they stopped and picked me up. I was searched then taken back with them to be interviewed by someone from the Intelligence corps as to who I was and why I was walking inside their area.

I never felt under any threat from the Army or in any danger and was never badly treated partly of course because I had nothing to do with the situation, neither loyalist nor republican and I was not long out of the Army and so felt in good company, also because I had nothing to hide or anything to cover up.

On questioning I described why I was in Belfast, my

history, why I was walking through the area they patrolled and my analogy of the screen (divine ground) being the reality and space-time (which is in the 'here and now' sense Belfast) superimposed upon it.

After a while I was released but I was picked up similarly (by the same marines who were checking my story) and on another occasion by a foot patrol of the Parachute regiment. Also stopped in the street and questioned (and the details checked) in total about half a dozen times during my stay in Belfast (about 2 years).

One of the reasons I felt compromised and that my stay there was no longer so sensible was that I would be walking around as usual, and the Land Rover would pass, and they would know me and give me a friendly wave which to me was something I wished they wouldn't do.

My strategy was to merge with the screen (like blending in with the wallpaper) and because of these incidents I no longer had this sense of being anonymous.

I realised later that these areas were also patrolled by those who lived within the area. Once when walking into the 'Little Britain' area off the Crumlin Road adjacent to the Ardoyne, a car pulled up alongside me and I had to get in and then I was taken to a backstreet Union club.

There were two of them one of them was English, a Geordie by his accent which was surprising to me, I quickly found out it was a good guy/bad guy interview. I was answering questions from one of them and suddenly without any warning punched hard in the face by the other (Geordie playing the bad guy role) one.

Although as I have said previously, I am by no means a hard tough guy, I was and did remain calm, I think they were expecting me to be overcome with fear and to change my story and so on. I did realise how vulnerable I was because they were looking through my diary and I had my contacts, names and addresses etc. In there including Brian's address in Dublin (this was the ex-army friend I visited from where I made my first visit to Belfast) this was not good for me since it reinforced their idea that I was one of them (IRA), so to speak.

However perhaps my explanation of having been in the Army and that Brian was in the same troop, and I had helped him as friend (he had a very strong drinking habit and had a breakdown, delusions and the DT's and after this he realised it was seriously bad and started to attend AA meetings which I went along to with him), then later I helped him to buy himself out so explaining all this and so on may have convinced them that I was not in the IRA (and nor was he). I was hit several times and it did occur to me that I could be found in a ditch shot, as had happened from time to time to others.

I was let go, and though this was a relief, thereafter I could not feel the same i.e., my details, where I lived and so on (my address was more or less in the Republicans area) was now known to them. Just letting someone else know, innocently, my address as I have mentioned earlier ended up with me being in hospital. After this incident I always felt someone could come round at anytime if perhaps they had suspicions that my story wasn't good enough.

I saw an advert for a Nursing Assistant vacancy at the 'Royal Victoria' hospital and decided to leave the Post Office this was partly because the Post Office walks were very long in terms of distance covered. The Walk I was on and had been for a month or two involved me walking down the full length of the 'New Lodge Road' to get onto 'Shore Road' to then get a bus out a mile or so to the area that was my Walk, which seemed several miles long.

The main reason, however, was that I thought the job in the hospital in the 'Special Clinic' was 'Special' because of the sectarian situation in Belfast. It was however just the standard name given to a Sexually Transmitted Diseases (STD) clinic. I didn't realise this until after having been showed around.

Working there I felt I had a special insight to everything going on and that it was not sordid at all, in fact it was quite a spiritual experience.

It was, for sure, one of the most neutral places in Belfast where being Protestant or Republican didn't have any relevance, the standard practice in these clinics was to register the patient when he first turned up and then, after taking all the usual details in private, to issue him with a number. This was his (or her, the ladies clinic was next door) identity from then on.

The initial process was for the patient to see the consultant in his room (at times I would be present in the room to help e.g., to carry out the 2-urine test) some patients when they took off their jacket revealed that they were armed and this was ignored, whether the patient was Army, Police, IRA or whatever that the patient being armed was just accepted.

Then the patient would be seen by me in a cubicle so I could take bloods and a specimen by inserting a looped probe high up inside their urethra, then this l applied to a glass slide and solutions were applied to stain and fix the slide.

Following this I examined the slide under the microscope to look for the signs of VD e.g., for Gonorrhoea you would look for pairs of red kidney shaped diplococci, if the patient had a chancre (a painless ulcer) a specimen from this would be treated in a different way and examined to see if 'spirochetes' were present i.e., Syphilis.

When anything was found to indicate Gonorrhoea, NSU or Syphilis the consultant was fetched to look through the microscope to confirm the diagnosis.

The patient would then go back to see the consultant in his room where everything was explained and the treatment described and it was explained what the patient had to do until he was cured (no sex, no drinking).

An appointment card was given for him to notify his wife, girlfriend, or the relevant contacts so they would also attend the clinic. The clinic was known or referred to with a neutral sounding name and many people attending would and did not know anything (from start to finish) about the real nature of what was going on or the conditions they were being seen about and treated for.

The patient would then be seen by me in the cubicle

again, to be treated usually this was antibiotics by injection. Because you could not on every occasion rely on the patient returning again to the clinic the full course of the antibiotics was given in one large dose (depot procaine penicillin) this involved 2 injections in total 8mls the antibiotic, being suspended in an oil substance, would be released into the system slowly over days, the whole treatment given in one visit.

The job itself was interesting, although I was not a registered nurse, I was taking blood specimens, tissue, and urethral specimens, preparing them for the microscope then examining them to make a diagnosis (confirmed by the consultant) and delivering the treatment by injection.

The job was satisfying in the sense that the patient may have been walking around with a urethral discharge for several days indicating a sexual transmitted disease and realising that he will have to go and present himself to explain and to be examined and so forth.

A lot of the people coming in were married and happily married, some for example had been working away from home for a long period, had had too much to drink one evening and then gone with someone and now feel they may have ruined everything; that their marriage was over.

For many others who were homosexual they were now in the position in having to make this public, to have to describe their sex life to others, be examined and so on.

Being in the position where you were taking all their details, being present to know their situation, taking the specimens and so on and yet being natural and accepting with them and showing that everything was quite normal was rewarding. When with the patient you could almost feel the tension, fear or whatever in them disappear due to the way they were being received and dealt with.

After only about 10 minutes they would be invited back in to see the consultant (following the diagnosis being made and the treatment ordered) and then return back to you to receive the treatment.

Their relief, at being seen and dealt with and knowing the measures that would be taken to ensure their wife, girlfriend, boyfriend and so on would also be dealt with, that their life had not come to an end, that their marriage was not ruined, was plain to see.

All this to me was quite spiritually rewarding and deepened my awareness that God is equally present within everyone, that the 'secret' is to love and respect God always in every situation.

Love and respect God (inwardly) and you experience love and respect.

Due to the experience of working in this clinic I decided to apply for nurse training which involved me taking an exam, I passed and was all set to begin a 4-year combined SRN and Psychiatric nursing course at The Royal Victoria Hospital.

The situation in Belfast was continuing with lots of unrest including a general strike which made life particularly difficult. I remember walking up Falls Road on the way to work at the hospital and weaving between the burnt-out car wrecks and rubble.

I could have started the training, but it would have meant being committed to staying in Belfast for at least 4 years, and as mentioned previously I no longer felt as anonymous and safe, since I was known about by the Army and also by the vigilanties (in the Crumlin / Ardoyne areas) so I returned to London and was accepted for a SRN course in a hospital there.

I was able to stay in a friend's house in Turnham Green, West London. After I arrived it was getting dark, and I went out to buy a takeaway.

I found the experience to be almost psychedelic, the streetlights were on, the shop windows were lit up, there was music playing; this was such a contrast to what I was used to in Belfast where there were no streetlights, and most windows were boarded up.

The next day on the bus I heard a girl talking behind me with a very pronounced Birmingham accent, I turned round and was surprised to find that she was West Indian however obviously born in England. I then felt that this was wonderful, the key perhaps to a peaceful society was to be found in having a mixture of nationalities so not in the danger that comes from the segregated 'Us and Them' tribal divisions that seemed to mark Belfast out at that time.

It is so much easier to be 'equal to all' as God or the 'Whole' is.

The Whole is within each Part.

The Whole is greater than the sum total of Parts.

The Whole remains the same independently of a change in the Parts.

56 Although neither Voyager spacecraft (Voyager 1 & Voyager 2) is heading toward any particular star, Voyager 1 will pass within 1.6 light-years' distance of the star Gliese 445, currently in the constellation Camelopardalis, in about 40,000 years.

Carl Sagan noted that "The spacecraft will be encountered, and the record played only if there are advanced space-faring civilizations in interstellar space, but the launching of this 'bottle' into the cosmic 'ocean' says something very hopeful about life on this planet."

en.wikipedia.org/wiki/Voyager_Golden_Record

Music From Earth

The following music was included on the Voyager record.

- Bach, Brandenburg Concerto No. 2 in F. First Movement, Munich Bach Orchestra, Karl Richter, conductor. 4:40
- Java, court gamelan, "Kinds of Flowers," recorded by Robert Brown. 4:43
- Senegal, percussion, recorded by Charles Duvelle. 2:08
- Zaire, Pygmy girls' initiation song, recorded by Colin Turnbull. 0:56
- Australia, Aborigine songs, "Morning Star" and "Devil Bird," recorded by Sandra LeBrun Holmes. 1:26
- Mexico, "El Cascabel," performed by Lorenzo Barcelata and the Mariachi México. 3:14

- "Johnny B. Goode," written and performed by Chuck Berry. 2:38
- New Guinea, men's house song, recorded by Robert MacLennan. 1:20
- Japan, shakuhachi, "Tsuru No Sugomori" ("Crane's Nest,") performed by Goro Yamaguchi. 4:51
- Bach, "Gavotte en rondeaux" from the Partita No. 3 in E major for Violin, performed by Arthur Grumiaux. 2:55
- Mozart, The Magic Flute, Queen of the Night aria, no. 14. Edda Moser, soprano. Bavarian State Opera, Munich, Wolfgang Sawallisch, conductor. 2:55
- Georgian S.S.R., chorus, "Tchakrulo," collected by Radio Moscow. 2:18
- Peru, panpipes, and drum, collected by Casa de la Cultura, Lima. 0:52
- "Melancholy Blues," performed by Louis Armstrong and his Hot Seven. 3:05
- Azerbaijan S.S.R., bagpipes, recorded by Radio Moscow. 2:30
- Stravinsky, Rite of Spring, Sacrificial Dance, Columbia Symphony Orchestra, Igor Stravinsky, conductor. 4:35
- Bach, The Well-Tempered Clavier, Book 2, Prelude and Fugue in C, No.1. Glenn Gould, piano. 4:48
- Beethoven, Fifth Symphony, First Movement, the Philharmonia Orchestra, Otto Klemperer, conductor. 7:20
- Bulgaria, "Izlel je Delyo Hagdutin," sung by Valya Balkanska. 4:59
- Navajo Indians, Night Chant, recorded by Willard Rhodes. 0:57
- Holborne, Paueans, Galliards, Almains and Other Short Aeirs, "The Fairie Round," performed by David Munrow and the Early Music Consort of London. 1:17
- Solomon Islands, panpipes, collected by the Solomon Islands Broadcasting Service. 1:12
- Peru, wedding song, recorded by John Cohen. 0:38

- China, ch'in, "Flowing Streams," performed by Kuan P'ing-hu. 7:37
- India, raga, "Jaat Kahan Ho," sung by Surshri Kesar Bai Kerkar. 3:30
- "Dark Was the Night," performed by Blind Willie Johnson. 3:15
- Beethoven, String Quartet No. 13 in B flat, Opus 130, Cavatina, performed by Budapest String Quartet. 6:37

Voyager.jpl.nasa.gov/goldenrecord/whats on the record/music/

Johann Sebastian Bach (1685-1750) was not a mathematician in a strict sense of the word. There is no "Bach convergence theorem" in real analysis, nor is there a "Bach isomorphism theorem" in algebra. Bach had no formal training in mathematics beyond elementary arithmetic. But, as we will see, Bach was definitely a mathematician in a more general sense, as a composer whose works are replete with patterns, structures, recursions, and other precisely crafted features. There are even hints of Fibonacci numbers and the golden ratio in Bach's music. Indeed, in this larger sense, Bach arguably reigns supreme over all classical composers as a "mathematician," although Mozart is a close second.

Mathematics and music

Just as some of the best musicians and composers are "mathematical," so too many of the best mathematicians are quite musical. It is quite common at evening receptions of large mathematical conferences to be serenaded by concert-quality musical performers, who, in their day jobs, are accomplished mathematicians of some renown.

Albert Einstein playing his violin.

Perhaps the best real-life example of a mathematician-musician was Albert Einstein, who was also an accomplished pianist and violinist. His second wife Elsa recalled how Albert, during deep concentration on a mathematical problem, would often sit down with a piano or violin and play for a while, then return to his work. Once, after a two-week period of intense research interspersed with random music playing, Einstein emerged with the first working draft of his paper on general relativity. He later said, "If ... I were not a physicist; I would probably be a musician. I often think in music. I live my daydreams in music. I see my life in terms of music."

So, who were Einstein's two favourite composers? You guessed it — Bach and Mozart.

The golden ratio and Fibonacci numbers in Bach's music
Perhaps the most remarkable "mathematics" in Bach's music are the instances of the golden ratio, usually denoted with the Greek letter $\varnothing$ = (1 + sqrt (5))/2 = 1.6180339887..., together with the Fibonacci numbers, whose limiting ratio is equal to $\varnothing$ (i.e., the Greek letter phi).
https://mathscholar.org/2021/06/bach-as-mathematician

The golden ratio defines the harmony of most objects and, thus, is the most perfect expression of beauty.
The section aurea, or golden ratio, is the essence of many artistic works. We can easily find it in architecture, painting, and sculpture, which use the pattern to achieve an ideal symmetry.

From the leaves that grow on trees to the spirals in pinecones and the geometric formations of snowflakes and the dynamic of black holes and galactic dimensions, the biological configurations of our universe follow this enigmatic algorithm that defines the perfect harmony of most objects. And the most wonderful part of this model is that it can be replicated by the arts. Applying this pattern to musical composition is especially attractive since it is easily done, and the result is sublime.

Since the dawn of mankind, the golden ratio has always been close to music: certain theories suggest that, guided by the golden ratio, Pythagoras discovered the resonance of notes on a taut string, and that Plato used this knowledge to create his theory on the Music of the Spheres. If we jump ahead to the 20th century, we find György Ligeti, who dared to compose "Apparitions", a song divided into sections that were proportional to the golden ratio.

In sum, the golden ratio is no more than the mathematical translation of an algorithm used by nature, and that stands out because of its hyper-harmonic condition; that is, it is a lesson on aesthetic perfection, courtesy of the natural world
Faena.com/aleph/how-to-compose-a-song-with-the-golden-ratio-and-the-fibonacci-sequence

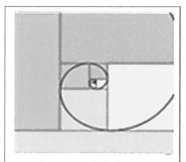

The shape is infinitely repeated when magnified.

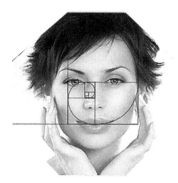

57 But what is clear is that people thought about it far less often than the seven-second myth suggests.
They recorded a sexual thought in the last half hour on approximately 4% of occasions, which works out as about once per day, compared with 19 reported in the Fisher studyThe real shock from Hoffman's study is the relative unimportance of sex in the participants' thoughts. People said they thought more about food, sleep, personal hygiene, social contact, time off, and (until about 5pm) coffee. Watching TV, checking email and other forms of media use also won out over sex for the entire day. In fact, sex only became a predominant thought towards the end of the day (around midnight), and even then, it was firmly in second place, behind sleep.
ww.bbc.com/future/article/20140617-how-often-do-men-think-about-sex

58 Someone told me it stands for a backward **BOY** hence **YOB.**

59 Vision begins with light passing through the cornea and the lens, which combine to produce a clear image of the visual world on a sheet of photoreceptors called the retina. As in a camera, the image on the retina is reversed: Objects above the center project to the lower part and vice versa. The information from the retina — in the form of electrical signals — is sent via the optic nerve to other parts of the brain, which ultimately process the image and allow us to see.
Hearing is over a small range of frequencies (vibrations) i.e., from 20 Hz to 17 KHz. Seeing however, is in the visible region of the electromagnetic spectrum, from 3.8 $x10^{14}$ centimetres per second (cps) [red] to 7.7x10^{14} cps [violet]. Radiation reflects off a physical object, say it is a bowl of fruit, and then strikes the eyes

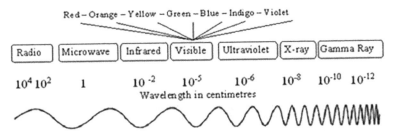

resulting in visual perception. The brain's visual system processes the multitude of reflected frequencies into different shades and hues and through this not-entirely-understood psychophysical phenomenon: most people perceive a bowl of fruit.

Because the frequencies of visible light are such high numbers, for convenience the wavelengths are used instead i.e., from 700 nanometres (red) to 400 nanometres (violet). Radio waves, visible light, X-rays, and all other parts of the spectrum are fundamentally the same thing i.e., electromagnetic radiation.

Electromagnetic radiation can be described as a stream of photons (massless particles) each travelling in a wave-like pattern at the speed of light. Each photon contains a certain amount of energy, the only difference between the various types of electromagnetic radiation e.g., radio waves, microwaves, infrared, visible light, ultraviolet, X-rays and so on is in the energy of the photons, in radio waves they have low energies, in gamma-rays they have the high energies.

The electromagnetic spectrum can be expressed in terms of frequency (e.g., KHz, MHz), wavelength (e.g., nanometres, microns) or energy (electron volts eV, KeV) (Because of the high numbers involved e.g., 10 followed by 14 0's, the wavelength or energy values are used)

Electromagnetic radiation -Wikipedia

60 An appearance of God, or spirit, in physical form (OUP dictionary).

61 If I were to have a stroke, I could very likely lose consciousness of one side of my body and lose the ability to speak. This lack of consciousness is not because consciousness has been destroyed or modified; it is because of a destruction or disturbance in the relationship of parts (neurons in a part of the brain). Given the right treatment e.g. physiotherapy, speech therapy and time, I can possibly regain most or some of my previous mobility and power of speech i. e. the relationships in the remaining viable areas of the brain develop to replace and

take over the functions damaged by the stroke.

62 Knowledge is said to be a priori when it does not depend for its authority upon the evidence of experience
(The Oxford Companion to Philosophy 2nd edition OUP).

Milton Keynes UK
Ingram Content Group UK Ltd.
UKHW022201061023
430084UK00009B/89